THE OFFICIAL COOKBOOK

RECIPES FROM SUNNYDALE

THE OFFICIAL COOKBOOK

RECIPES FROM SUNNYDALE

By Kim Laidlaw

SAN RAFAEL • LOS ANGELES • LONDON

Contents

CHAPTER FOUR

MONSTROUS MAINS

CHAPTER FIVE

SWEET FANGS

CHAPTER SIX

DEMON DRINKS

INTRODUCTION

GILES: "For as long as there have been vampires, there has been the Slayer. One girl in all the world, a Chosen One . . ."

BUFFY: "He loves doing this part."

"THE HARVEST" (SEASON 1, EPISODE 2)

If you've ever wondered what kept the Slayerettes fueled through demon battles, school drama, and apocalyptic chaos, welcome to *Buffy the Vampire Slayer: Recipes from Sunnydale*—your guide to Sunnydale-inspired comfort food with a little bite.

This isn't your basic cookbook. It's a Slayer's survival guide, packed with recipes that honor the quippy chaos and supernatural charm of *Buffy the Vampire Slayer*. From patrol-night snacks to desserts that would make Anya forget about bunnies, these dishes are designed for anyone who's faced the wacky and lived to tell the tale. Some meals bring the cozy while others bring the wiggins, but in the end, they are all slay-worthy.

Start your morning with the Dawn of the Day chapter, chock-full of breakfast staples. Whether you're recharging after late-night slayage or just avoiding vampy vibes before coffee, options such as Big Bad Breakfast Burrito (page 21) and Strawberry Toaster Tart Temptations (page 19) will get you from groggy to five by five.

Need fuel between demon attacks or awkward encounters in Dateville? The Bites chapter has you covered, with Hot (Buffalo) Wings from Hell (page 32) and Spellbound Nachos (page 40), perfect for midnight stakeouts or research parties.

Lunchtime is personal. In "Let's Do Lunch," dive into emotionally complex comfort foods such as Soulless Tortilla Soup (page 68) or the Cheese Man Melt (page 62), all before dinner takes a turn for the dramatic in Monstrous Mains. There you'll find Slay Day Garlic Veggie Noodles (page 100) and Family Spaghetti Dinner (page 77)—meals that channel Buffy's more grounded moments at home with Joyce and Dawn. Even the Doublemeat Palace Burgers (page 80) get a glow-up here, minus the mystery meat.

Sweets get their own spotlight in Sweet Fangs. Think Cursed Chocolate Bark (page 105), Angel's Food Cake (page 107), and Magical Chaos Cookies (page 108—dangerously good, but no spell required).

And finally, Demon Drinks offers refreshing, nonalcoholic options like The Love Spell (page 131) and The Bronze Brew (page 132). Perfect for rehydrating post-patrol or toasting another narrowly avoided apocalypse with your friends while rocking out to Dingoes Ate My Baby at the Bronze.

Sharpen your knives (and stakes), preheat your oven, and get ready to slay!

CHAPTER ONE

DAWN OF THE DAY

"A CRANKY SLAYER IS A CARELESS SLAYER."

—BUFFY TO GILES
"NEVER KILL A BOY ON A FIRST DATE" (SEASON 1, EPISODE 5)

Nothing fuels a Slayer and her Slayerettes like a good breakfast. Whether you need a boost after dusting vampires all night or you're looking for a hearty bite to keep you amped during Slayer training in the library, the recipes in this chapter bring the delicious.

the only
Classified
orbits of
it was
solar system.

MAKES 4 SERVINGS

"Bad Eggs" Breakfast Scramble

This breakfast scramble is a wild, flavor-packed dish that is a nod to one of Buffy's weirder high school assignments—caring for egg "babies" as a parenting exercise. But when the eggs hatch parasitic creatures, they become both literal and symbolic food gone bad. Don't worry, though, this spinach and spicy sausage scramble won't hatch anything . . . probably. "Normally, I'd say 'ew'. . . but 'ew.'"

Ingredients

8 large eggs

2 tablespoons whole milk

½ teaspoon kosher salt

¼ teaspoon freshly ground black pepper

2 teaspoons extra-virgin olive oil

6 ounces linguica, andouille, or other spicy smoked sausage, cubed (optional)

2 packed cups (about 3 ounces) chopped fresh baby spinach

2 green onions, white and green parts, minced

1 tablespoon unsalted butter

½ cup crumbled feta cheese

In a large bowl, whisk together the eggs, milk, salt, and pepper until thoroughly combined.

In a frying pan over medium heat, warm the oil. Add the sausage (if using) and cook, stirring occasionally, until lightly browned, about 3 minutes. Add the spinach and green onions, reduce the heat to medium-low, and cook, stirring occasionally, until the spinach is wilted, about 1 minute.

Add the butter to the pan. When the butter is melted, add the egg mixture and cook, stirring gently, until the eggs are barely cooked into moist curds. Add the cheese and stir to combine. Serve at once.

"OH NO, I ALMOST ATE ONE OF THESE THINGS . . . I THINK I FULFILLED MY GROSS-OUT QUOTA FOR THE DECADE."

—XANDER

"BAD EGGS" (SEASON 2, EPISODE 12)

MAKES 1 LOAF (6 TO 8 SERVINGS)

Peanut Butter–Banana Bread

Heartbreak sucks. After her breakup with Tara, Willow goes deep into dark magic, hanging with Amy and visiting Rack—a warlock who fuels magical highs. Willow wakes one morning after an out-of-control night of magic and cries in the shower, afterward conjuring Tara's clothes into a phantom embrace because she misses her so much. When she comes downstairs, Dawn tries to comfort her with her "own brand-new invention": peanut butter-and-banana quesadillas. This Peanut Butter–Banana Bread captures that same odd, heartfelt attempt to make things feel okay again.

Ingredients

Nonstick cooking spray

1½ cups all-purpose flour

1½ teaspoons baking powder

¼ teaspoon baking soda

½ teaspoon ground cinnamon

½ teaspoon kosher salt

3 very ripe bananas, peeled

2 large eggs

¾ cup packed light brown sugar

¼ cup sour cream

¼ cup creamy peanut butter (unsweetened)

1 teaspoon pure vanilla extract

3 tablespoons unsalted butter, melted

½ cup chocolate chips, plus more for garnish (optional)

Preheat the oven to 350°F. Grease a 9-by-5-inch loaf pan with cooking spray. Line the pan with a piece of parchment paper so the long edges overhang the pan by 1 or 2 inches (this helps the bread slide out of the pan more easily).

In a medium bowl, whisk together the flour, baking powder, baking soda, cinnamon, and salt. In a large bowl, using the back of a fork, mash the bananas to a smooth purée. Add the eggs, brown sugar, sour cream, peanut butter, vanilla, and melted butter to the bowl with the banana purée and stir to combine. Add the flour mixture and stir to combine. Stir in the chocolate chips (if using).

Spoon the batter into the prepared pan. Bake until deeply golden brown and a toothpick inserted into the center of the loaf comes out clean, about 1 hour 15 minutes. Immediately sprinkle the hot bread with additional chocolate chips (if using). Let cool for 20 minutes in the pan set on a wire rack. Then, using the parchment handles, remove the bread from the pan and place it onto the rack to cool completely before slicing.

"I'M MAKING PEANUT BUTTER-AND-BANANA QUESADILLAS. YOU WANT?"

—DAWN
"WRECKED" (SEASON 6, EPISODE 10)

KISS
THE

MAKES 8 TO 9 SCONES

Watcher Earl Grey Tea Scones

Proper, sensible . . . and undeniably British, these Earl Grey scones are a tribute to Giles—Watcher extraordinaire and the tweedy, always-refined anchor of the Slayerettes. Flavored with fragrant Earl Grey and bright orange zest, the scones are classic with a twist, just like him. Even after a near-death experience, when Spike mocks his preference for tea even in dire circumstances, he keeps calm and carries on . . . with tea, of course. Add a handful of dried currants if you fancy.

Ingredients

Scones

1 cup heavy cream

2 Earl Grey tea bags

2 cups all-purpose flour, plus more for dusting

1/3 cup granulated sugar

2 teaspoons baking powder

½ teaspoon kosher salt

4 tablespoons chilled unsalted butter, diced

Finely grated zest of 1 orange, divided

1 large egg

Glaze

1 cup powdered sugar

1 tablespoon freshly squeezed orange juice

Special Equipment

2½- to 3-inch fluted or round cutter

> "OH, POOR WATCHER. HAS YOUR LIFE PASSED BEFORE YOUR EYES? CUPPA TEA? CUPPA TEA?
>
> —SPIKE
> "BARGAINING, PART 1"
> (SEASON 6, EPISODE 1)

At least 1 hour before making the scones, in a small saucepan over low heat, warm the cream just until steaming; do not let it boil. Remove the pan from the heat, add 1 tea bag, cover, and set aside to steep for 10 minutes. Remove the tea bag, pour the cream into a jar or bowl, and refrigerate until cold, at least 1 hour or up to overnight.

Position a rack in the upper third of the oven and preheat the oven to 400°F. Line a large, rimmed baking sheet with parchment paper.

TO MAKE THE SCONES: In a large bowl, combine the flour, granulated sugar, baking powder, and salt and stir to combine. Add the butter and, using a pastry blender or two knives, cut the butter into the flour mixture until the mixture resembles coarse meal. Cut open the remaining tea bag and add the leaves to the mixture along with 1 teaspoon of the orange zest. Stir to combine.

Set aside 2 tablespoons of the chilled cream. In a small bowl, whisk together the egg and the remaining chilled cream until blended. Pour the egg mixture into the flour mixture and stir just until the dough comes together.

Turn the dough out onto a lightly floured work surface and press into a ball. Press the dough into a round ¾ to 1 inch thick. Using a 2½- to 3-inch fluted or round cutter, cut the dough into as many rounds as you can. Press the scraps together, press out the dough again, and cut more rounds. You should have 8 or 9 scones.

Transfer the scones to the prepared baking sheet, spacing them evenly. Bake the scones until lightly golden, 13 to 15 minutes. While the scones are baking, make the glaze.

TO MAKE THE GLAZE: In a medium or large bowl, whisk together the powdered sugar with the reserved cream and the orange juice.

Transfer the scones to a wire rack and let cool for about 15 minutes, then brush generously with the glaze. Sprinkle with the remaining orange zest. Let cool, then serve.

MAKES 16 DOUGHNUTS, PLUS HOLES

Deceitful Jelly Doughnuts

These jelly-filled doughnuts lure you in with their warm, sugary coating and surprise with their jammy, blood-red centers. Raspberry, cherry, or strawberry—take your pick! In "The Zeppo" from Season 3, as Giles leaves to try to contact the spirit guides, he stops to grab a doughnut on the way out, and the following hilarious exchange ensues:

"Did you want a jelly?" Buffy asks.

"I always have a jelly. I'm always the one that says, 'Let's have a jelly in the mix,'" Giles says.

Just don't let Buffy get to them first . . . she already had three.

Ingredients

1 cup whole milk, warmed (110°F)

1 envelope (2¼ teaspoons) instant yeast

2½ cups all-purpose flour, plus more for dusting

¾ cup sugar, divided

2 large egg yolks

1 teaspoon kosher salt

4 tablespoons unsalted butter, at room temperature

Canola oil, for frying

One 13-ounce jar of your favorite jam (about 1½ cups), such as raspberry

Special Equipment

Stand mixer with dough hook attachment

Deep-fry thermometer

3-inch round cutter

1½-inch round cutter (optional)

Piping bag and small tip

"NO, NO, NO. LET'S RUN THAT UP TO FOUR JELLIES."

—XANDER, "THE ZEPPO" (SEASON 3, EPISODE 13)

In the bowl of a stand mixer, whisk together the milk and yeast. Set aside for 5 minutes, or until foamy. Add the flour, ¼ cup of the sugar, the egg yolks, and salt. Fit the mixer with the dough hook attachment and mix just until combined. Add the butter and mix on medium speed until the butter is completely absorbed and the dough relaxes, about 5 minutes. The dough will be soft and sticky. Cover the bowl with plastic wrap and refrigerate for at least 1 hour and up to 12 hours.

Line a baking sheet with parchment paper and dust it with flour. Roll out the dough on a lightly floured surface to ½ inch thick. Using a 3-inch plain round cutter, cut out as many rounds as possible; you should have about 16. (If you want to use the scraps, press them together and roll out into ½-inch thickness and cut out doughnut holes using a 1½-inch round cutter.)

Place the doughnut rounds about 1 inch apart on the prepared baking sheet and cover loosely with plastic wrap. Let rest in a warm spot until they have almost doubled in size, about 30 minutes.

Meanwhile, fill a heavy-bottomed pot with at least 2 inches of oil. Heat over medium-high heat until a deep-fry thermometer registers 350°F. Line a large wire rack with paper towels and set it next to the stovetop.

When the oil is to temperature, carefully add a few doughnut rounds to the oil, taking care not to overcrowd the pot. Fry, turning a few times, until light golden brown and cooked through, 4 to 5 minutes. Using a slotted spoon, transfer the doughnuts to the prepared rack. Repeat with the remaining doughnuts and holes, adjusting the heat to keep the temperature consistent.

To fill the doughnuts, using a paring knife, carefully carve a small opening in the side of each round, forming a cavity. Put the jam in a piping bag fitted with a small tip, or a plastic bag with a small corner cut out. Pipe jam into each doughnut round.

Fill a shallow bowl with the remaining ½ cup sugar and toss the filled doughnuts in the sugar until evenly coated. Serve.

"What were you dreaming about
"I was dreaming that they
"A what?"
"You know. A zannibar." I
wrong word, her voice was so
"What's that?"
I never felt

"TO MAKE YOU A VAMPIRE, THEY HAVE TO SUCK YOUR BLOOD, AND THEN YOU HAVE TO SUCK THEIR BLOOD. IT'S LIKE A WHOLE BIG SUCKING THING."
—BUFFY
"WELCOME TO THE HELLMOUTH" (SEASON 1, EPISODE 1)

MAKES 6 TOASTER TARTS

Strawberry Toaster Tart Temptation

In Sunnydale, even breakfast isn't safe. These flaky, jam-filled pastries might look like any teenager's sugary go-to for breakfast—but their blood-red centers say otherwise. Just like the vampires blending in with students in the high school halls, these tarts are sweet on the outside, with a sinister heart. The kind of treat you'd crave before patrol . . . or after a late-night bite. Temptation never tasted so deadly.

Ingredients

Tarts

All-purpose flour, for dusting

2 sheets frozen puff pastry (17 ounces), thawed but very cold

1 large egg beaten with 1 teaspoon water, for egg wash

½ cup strawberry jam (or your favorite jam)

Glaze

1 cup powdered sugar, plus more as needed

2 tablespoons whole milk, plus more as needed

¼ teaspoon pure vanilla extract

Red gel food coloring, for tinting (optional)

Line a baking sheet with parchment paper.

TO MAKE THE TARTS: On a lightly floured work surface, gently roll out one sheet of puff pastry into a 10-by-12-inch rectangle. Using a sharp paring knife, cut the pastry into 6 equal rectangles. Repeat with the second sheet of puff pastry for a total of 12 rectangles.

Place half of the pastry rectangles on the prepared baking sheet, spacing them apart. Place a piece of parchment on top and lay the other pastries on top. Refrigerate for 30 minutes.

Remove the pastries from the refrigerator and set the top layer of pastries aside. Brush the border of each of the 6 rectangles on the baking sheet lightly with egg wash. Spread about 1½ tablespoons jam over each rectangle, leaving a ½-inch border on all sides. Top each jam-topped rectangle with one of the plain pastry rectangles. Press the edges firmly to seal (gently pressing out any air), then use the tines of a fork to crimp the edges. Use a pizza cutter or knife to neaten up the edges so they are even. Refrigerate the pastries while you preheat the oven.

Preheat the oven to 400°F. Pierce the tops of the pastries all over with the fork. Brush the tops of the pastries all over lightly with the egg wash. Bake until golden brown and crisp, about 20 minutes. Transfer to a wire rack to cool completely.

TO MAKE THE GLAZE: In a medium or large bowl, whisk together the powdered sugar, milk, and vanilla to form a smooth, thick mixture. If the mixture is too thick, add a little milk; if it's too thin, add a little more powdered sugar. Add red food coloring (if using) to all the glaze or divide the glaze and add coloring just to some to create bloody drips on top of the pastries.

When the pastries are completely cool, spread the glaze over the tops, leaving the borders uncovered. Dribble with the blood-red glaze and swirl with a toothpick, if you like.

MAKES 1 DOZEN DOUGHNUTS

Midnight Baked Doughnuts

Sweet tooth much? These baked cinnamon doughnuts dusted with powdered sugar pay homage to the many doughnut runs scattered throughout the series. Favored by Willow, Xander, Buffy, and Giles (among other characters), doughnuts offer a comforting constant amid the chaos of Sunnydale. Whether fueling late-night patrols or easing tense moments, these sweet treats are a beloved indulgence for the Slayerettes.

Ingredients

Nonstick cooking spray

1½ cups all-purpose flour

½ packed cup dark brown sugar

1½ teaspoons baking powder

1 teaspoon ground cinnamon

¾ teaspoon kosher salt

⅔ cup whole milk, at room temperature

2 large eggs, at room temperature

2 tablespoons canola oil

2 teaspoons pure vanilla extract

½ cup powdered sugar

Special Equipment

Two 6-cup nonstick doughnut pans

Piping bag and medium round tip

Preheat the oven to 350°F. Spray two 6-cup nonstick doughnut pans generously with cooking spray.

In a large bowl, whisk together the flour, brown sugar, baking powder, cinnamon, and salt. In another bowl, whisk together the milk, eggs, oil, and vanilla. Pour the wet ingredients into the dry ingredients and whisk until just combined.

Transfer the batter to a piping bag fitted with a medium round tip. Pipe the batter into each doughnut cup, dividing evenly and filling each about three-quarters full.

Bake until a toothpick inserted into a doughnut comes out clean, 8 to 10 minutes. Invert the doughnuts onto a wire rack; if they are resistant, run a knife around the edge to loosen them.

Put the powdered sugar into a bowl. Gently toss each doughnut in the powdered sugar to coat, then return to the wire rack. Put any remaining powdered sugar into a small fine-mesh sieve and dust the tops of the doughnuts. Serve at once, while still warm.

"I'LL PACK SOME FOOD. WHO ELSE LIKES POWDERED DOUGHNUTS?"

—WILLOW
"SOME ASSEMBLY REQUIRED"
(SEASON 2, EPISODE 2)

MAKES 4 BURRITOS

Big Bad Breakfast Burrito

Named for the "Big Bad" (the ultimate villain that Buffy and the Slayerettes face each season) and inspired by Buffy's fearless stand against the Master in the Season 1 episode "Prophecy Girl," this breakfast burrito is packed with flavor and attitude and is bold enough to take on any appetite. Don't wig out—you can skip the bacon for a vegetarian twist or go full throttle with spicy sauteéd chorizo.

Ingredients

1 medium russet potato, diced

1 tablespoon kosher salt, plus more for seasoning

4 thick-cut bacon slices, chopped

½ small yellow onion, finely chopped

1 tablespoon neutral oil, such as canola

Freshly ground black pepper

6 large eggs

2 tablespoons whole milk

4 large (10- to 12-inch) flour tortillas, preferably tomato red, warmed

Your favorite salsa, for serving

½ cup shredded Monterey Jack or cheddar cheese

Put the diced potato in a saucepan and add enough cold water to cover. Add 1 tablespoon salt. Bring to a boil over high heat, stirring occasionally. Reduce the heat to medium-low and simmer until just tender when pierced with the tip of a knife, about 5 minutes. Drain and set aside.

In a large frying pan over medium heat, cook the bacon, stirring, until crisp and browned, about 5 minutes. Using a slotted spoon, transfer the bacon to paper towels to drain. Pour off all but about 1 tablespoon bacon fat. Add the onion and a pinch of salt and cook over medium heat, stirring, until softened and browned, about 4 minutes. Add the diced potatoes and a drizzle of oil, season with salt and pepper, and continue to cook, stirring occasionally, until crisp and golden, about 5 minutes.

Meanwhile, in a large bowl, whisk together the eggs, milk, and a pinch each of salt and pepper until thoroughly blended. Reduce the heat to low and add the egg mixture to the pan along with the bacon. Cook, stirring occasionally, until the eggs are cooked to your liking.

Fill the tortillas with equal amounts of the potato-egg mixture, top with a spoonful of salsa, and sprinkle with cheese. Roll into a burrito and serve at once, with more salsa on the side.

"I FEEL STRONG. I FEEL DIFFERENT. LET'S GO."

—BUFFY
"PROPHECY GIRL" (SEASON 1, EPISODE 12)

MAKES 18 MUFFINS

Triple Berry Mayhem Muffins

Packed with three kinds of juicy berries and plenty of charm, these muffins are perfect when facing tough questions—just like Buffy and her gang endure when the Watchers' Council launches an intense review of her skills and methods. As secrets about Glory and her origin as a god from a Hell dimension emerge, these sweet, persuasive treats help steady their nerves during high-stakes scrutiny. Feeling saucy? Add extra berries on top for a little flair.

Ingredients

2 cups all-purpose flour

2 teaspoons baking powder

½ teaspoon baking soda

1½ teaspoons kosher salt

2 large eggs

1 cup sour cream

⅓ cup canola oil

⅓ cup sugar, plus more for sprinkling

Finely grated zest of 1 lemon

½ cup fresh blueberries

½ cup fresh raspberries

½ cup chopped fresh blackberries

Special Equipment

Two 12-cup muffin pans

Paper liners

Preheat the oven to 400°F. Line 18 cups of two standard 12-cup muffin pans with paper liners.

In a medium bowl, sift together the flour, baking powder, baking soda, and salt. In a large bowl, whisk together the eggs, sour cream, oil, sugar, and lemon zest until well combined. Add the dry ingredients and the blueberries, raspberries, and blackberries to the egg mixture and stir just until evenly moistened. The batter will be thick.

Scoop the batter into the prepared muffin cups, filling them about two-thirds full. Sprinkle the muffins with sugar.

Bake until the muffins are golden brown and a toothpick inserted into the center of one comes out clean, about 18 minutes. Let the muffins cool in the pans on a wire rack for 5 minutes, then unmold onto the rack. Enjoy warm or at room temperature.

"MUFFIN? I COOKED THEM MYSELF!"

—ANYA
"CHECKPOINT" (SEASON 5, EPISODE 12)

MAKES 4 SERVINGS (ABOUT 12 SMALL PANCAKES)

Sweet Serenity Pancakes

What's sweeter than two witches in love? Pancakes. Light and sweet like Willow and Tara's relationship, these lemon ricotta pancakes are tender and fluffy, with a bright citrus zing that lifts the spirit. As the gang struggles to cope with Buffy's death, Tara reminds Willow that "breakfast will make all things better." Together, they find comfort in this quiet, nurturing ritual.

Ingredients

- 16 ounces whole-milk ricotta cheese
- ½ cup all-purpose flour
- 3 large eggs, separated
- ¼ cup granulated sugar
- 2 tablespoons unsalted butter, melted
- Finely grated zest of 1 large lemon
- 2 tablespoons freshly squeezed lemon juice
- ¼ teaspoon kosher salt
- Canola oil, for cooking
- Sliced fresh strawberries or other berries (or mixed berries), for serving
- Powdered sugar, for serving

In a medium bowl, whisk together the ricotta, flour, egg yolks, granulated sugar, melted butter, lemon zest, lemon juice, and salt. In another bowl, using an electric mixer, beat the egg whites on high speed until soft peaks form. Gently and evenly fold the egg whites into the batter.

Heat a well-seasoned griddle or large nonstick frying pan over medium-low heat until hot. Lightly oil the griddle with canola oil. For each pancake, pour about ¼ cup batter onto the griddle and cook until the bottom is well-browned. Carefully turn the pancakes and cook until deeply golden on the second side, about 6 minutes total cooking time. (If the pancakes aren't cooking quickly enough, increase the heat, but if they start to get too dark, decrease the heat.) Transfer to a platter. Repeat until all the batter is used, oiling the griddle as needed.

Serve the pancakes topped with sliced strawberries and a dusting of powdered sugar.

"OOH, PANCAKES COULD GO IN BELLIES."

—WILLOW

"BECOMING, PART 1" (SEASON 6, EPISODE 1)

MAKES 4 SERVINGS (ABOUT 12 PANCAKES)

Perfect Coffee Pancakes with Mocha Syrup

What happens when everyone is suddenly swooning over Jonathan? Buffy does her Slayer thing and finds out his sudden fame is thanks to a spell that makes him appear to everyone as a beloved and flawless hero. In this magical reality, he doesn't make the coffee anymore—everyone else makes it for him (and fawns all over him as well). In fact, when Buffy seeks his relationship advice, she dutifully prepares his cup, adding cream and sugar to perfection. These coffee- and cocoa-flavored pancakes with mocha syrup capture the same comfort he conjures in that too-good-to-be-true world.

Ingredients

Cocoa–Coffee Pancakes

2 cups all-purpose flour

3 tablespoons sugar

2 tablespoons Dutch-process cocoa powder

2 teaspoons baking powder

2 teaspoons instant espresso powder

½ teaspoon kosher salt

1 cup whole milk

2 large eggs

4 tablespoons unsalted butter, melted, plus more for cooking

2 teaspoons pure vanilla extract

Mocha Syrup

½ cup chocolate sauce

1 teaspoon instant espresso powder

Toppings

Whipped cream (optional)

Cocoa powder (optional)

TO MAKE THE COCOA-COFFEE PANCAKES: In a large bowl, whisk together the flour, sugar, cocoa powder, baking powder, espresso powder, and salt. In a medium bowl, whisk together the milk, eggs, melted butter, and vanilla. Add the egg mixture to the flour mixture and stir until incorporated; the batter should be slightly lumpy.

Preheat the oven to 200°F and place a baking sheet in the oven (to keep the pancakes warm as you make them).

TO MAKE THE MOCHA SYRUP: In a small saucepan over low heat, stir together the chocolate sauce and espresso powder until the espresso powder is dissolved. Do not let the mixture boil. Set aside.

Heat a griddle or a large frying pan over medium heat. Coat generously with melted butter and then ladle about ¼ cup batter onto the griddle for each pancake. Cook until the edges are golden and bubbles form on the surface, then flip the pancakes and continue cooking until cooked through, about 3 minutes total. Reduce the heat to medium-low if the pancakes are cooking too quickly. Keep the finished pancakes warm in the oven while you cook the remaining pancakes.

TO FINISH: Serve the pancakes drizzled with mocha syrup and topped with whipped cream (if using) and a dusting of cocoa powder (if using).

"SO, WE'RE SAYING HE DID A SPELL JUST TO MAKE US THINK HE WAS COOL?"

—XANDER
"SUPERSTAR" (SEASON 4, EPISODE 17)

MAKES 1 SMOOTHIE

Slayer Smoothie

Time to get buff. Here's a smooth, energizing smoothie perfect for Slayers on the go. Creamy, rich, and subtly sweet, it packs a powerful nutritional punch with its hidden greens and warming spices. It might look like something that crawled out of the Hellmouth, but you can be assured that it's perfectly slayer-worthy. Quick to make and easy to customize with protein powder or ground flaxseed, this boost-ready drink fuels you through patrols and battles alike.

Ingredients

1 cup fresh baby spinach

1 large ripe frozen banana, peeled and chopped

½ cup nondairy milk or milk of your choice

2 tablespoons smooth peanut butter, almond butter, or sunflower butter

1 date, pitted and chopped

1 teaspoon unsweetened cocoa powder

Pinch of ground cinnamon, plus more for dusting (optional)

Special Equipment

Blender

In a blender, combine the spinach, banana, milk, peanut butter, date, cocoa powder, and cinnamon. Blend on high speed until thick and creamy, scraping down the sides of the blender jar as needed. Pour into a glass and serve, dusted with a little more cinnamon if you like.

"STRONG IS FIGHTING! IT'S HARD, AND IT'S PAINFUL, AND IT'S EVERY DAY. IT'S WHAT WE HAVE TO DO. AND WE CAN DO IT TOGETHER."

—BUFFY
"AMENDS" (SEASON 3, EPISODE 10)

CHAPTER TWO

"I KNOW WHAT YOU'RE THINKING, BUT DON'T WORRY. I DON'T BITE."

—ANGEL

"WELCOME TO THE HELLMOUTH"

(SEASON 1, EPISODE 1)

Angel might be off the blood, but that doesn't mean you have to skip snack time. From vamp-fighting fuel to Slayerettes movie-night munchies, this chapter's got all the eats you need for quality slay-time hangage. Whether you're post-patrol, mid-research, or just curled up with a broody vampire, these bites totally deliver.

MAKES 6 SERVINGS

Hot (Buffalo) Wings from Hell

These wings are hot, messy, and just a little dangerous—perfect for late-night dealings with a certain bleached-blonde vampire. When Buffy asks Spike how he killed two Slayers, he won't spill until he's got something in return: cash . . . and a plate of spicy Buffalo wings. Crisp, fiery, and slathered in buttery hot sauce, these are wings worthy of a backroom deal at the Bronze. They're best enjoyed while swapping dark secrets—or fending off one of Spike's infuriating quips. After all, he's always been bad.

Ingredients

Chicken Wings

3 pounds chicken wings and/or drummettes

1½ tablespoons baking powder

1 teaspoon garlic powder

1 teaspoon kosher salt

½ teaspoon cayenne pepper (optional)

½ teaspoon freshly ground black pepper

Sauce

2 tablespoons unsalted butter

½ cup hot pepper sauce, such as Frank's RedHot®, plus more for serving

2 teaspoons honey

Accompaniments

Blue cheese dressing

Celery sticks

TO MAKE THE CHICKEN WINGS: Position a rack in the upper third of the oven and preheat the oven to 425°F. Line a rimmed baking sheet with aluminum foil, then set a wire rack in the lined baking sheet. Dry the wings well with paper towels.

In a medium bowl, toss together the baking powder, garlic powder, salt, cayenne pepper, and black pepper. Add the wings and toss to evenly coat.

Arrange the wings skin side up on the prepared rack in an even layer and not touching one another. Bake, turning once after about 20 minutes, then again after another 10 minutes, until the wings are crisp, browned, and cooked through, about 35 minutes total.

TO MAKE THE SAUCE: Set a frying pan large enough to hold all the wings over medium heat. Melt the butter, then add the hot pepper sauce and honey and stir until combined. Set aside.

When the wings are cooked, let them sit on the rack for 5 minutes, then add the wings to the sauce. Toss to coat evenly. Transfer the wings to a platter and serve with the blue cheese dressing and celery sticks on the side.

THE BRONZE

"SPICY BUFFALO WINGS. ORDER ME UP A PLATE. I'M FEELING PECKISH."

—SPIKE

"FOOL FOR LOVE" (SEASON 5, EPISODE 7)

MAKES 1 DOZEN DEVILED EGGS

Demon Deviled Eggs

Buffy thinks flipping burgers at the Doublemeat Palace is rock bottom until Riley reappears with news of a Suvolte demon nesting somewhere in Sunnydale, its clutch of monstrous eggs threatening mass destruction. These deviled eggs may look like just food, but their cracked, blue-and-black-dyed whites evoke that evil spawn. Thankfully, their flavor is all comfort: creamy, dill-pickle filling with a satisfying tang. Inspired by Buffy's scramble to stop a hellish hatch, they're unsettlingly delicious and surprisingly crowd-pleasing.

Ingredients

6 large eggs

1/8 teaspoon black gel food coloring

3 tablespoons mayonnaise

2 teaspoons yellow mustard

1 packed tablespoon finely chopped dill pickle

Black sesame seeds, for garnish (optional)

Paprika, for garnish (optional)

Special Equipment

Piping bag and medium tip

Place the eggs into a medium saucepan and add water to cover by about 1 inch. Bring to a boil over high heat, then remove the pan from the heat, cover, and set aside for 10 minutes. Fill a medium bowl with ice and water and transfer the eggs to the ice water for 10 minutes to cool.

Remove the eggs from the water, pat them dry with paper towels, then gently roll the shells on the countertop to crack them all over, leaving the shells intact.

Pour out the ice water and add 3 cups of water to the bowl. Stir in the black food coloring, then submerge the eggs in the black water. Refrigerate the eggs for at least 2 hours or up to overnight.

Remove the eggs from the liquid and peel off and discard the shells. Halve the eggs lengthwise and scoop the yolks into a bowl. Arrange the egg whites, hollow sides up, on a platter.

Using the tines of a fork, smash the yolks until nearly smooth. Add the mayonnaise and mustard to the yolks and continue to mix until the mixture is smooth. Stir in the pickle. Transfer the yolk mixture to a piping bag fitted with a medium tip.

Pipe the yolk mixture into the egg-white halves, dividing it evenly. Garnish the stuffed eggs with the black sesame seeds (if using) and paprika (if using) and serve.

MAKES 4 SERVINGS

Mini Pizza Bagels

These Mini Pizza Bagels may look innocent, but they carry a sinister bite, much like Mrs. Summers's too-perfect and unsettling boyfriend, Ted. Although Buffy's friends fall for his charm (and his cooking), she knows something's off. Turns out, his drugged homemade pizzas are just one part of his creepy control tactics. These mini pizzas, however, are savory, satisfying, and perfect for a late-night snack.

Ingredients

- 4 mini bagels, split
- ½ cup pizza sauce
- ½ cup shredded low-moisture mozzarella cheese
- 1 teaspoon Italian seasoning
- ½ cup of your favorite pizza toppings, such as sliced black olives or chopped pepperoni

Position an oven rack in the upper third of the oven and preheat the oven to 425°F. Arrange the bagel halves, cut sides up, in an even layer on a baking sheet.

Spread 1 tablespoon of the sauce evenly over each bagel half. Divide the cheese among the bagel halves. Sprinkle each with a little Italian seasoning, then sprinkle evenly with the toppings of your choice.

Bake until the cheese is melted and the edges of the bagels are toasted and browned, 10 to 12 minutes. Let rest for a few minutes before diving in.

"PEOPLE ARE PERFECTLY HAPPY GETTING ALONG AND THEN VAMPIRES COME, AND THEY RUN AROUND, AND THEY KILL PEOPLE AND THEY TAKE OVER YOUR WHOLE HOUSE AND THEY START MAKING THESE STUPID MINI PIZZAS . . ."

—WILLOW
"TED" (SEASON 2, EPISODE 11)

MAKES ABOUT 1½ CUPS

Beer-Spiked Cheese Dip

This beer-spiked cheese dip is rich, sharp, and a little volatile, like the tension that erupts among the Slayerettes when Spike expertly stirs the pot. As old wounds and buried resentments rise to the surface, even Giles turns to drinking to quell the discomfort. Smooth and creamy, with just enough bite, this dip is perfect for sharing during uneasy alliances, last-minute plans, or whenever things feel a little too quiet for comfort.

Ingredients

2 tablespoons unsalted butter

1 small jalapeño, seeded and minced (optional)

2 tablespoons all-purpose flour

½ cup whole milk

⅓ cup lager- or pilsner-style beer, plus more as needed

4 ounces shredded sharp cheddar cheese

6 ounces American cheese, chopped

Tortilla chips or soft pretzels, for serving

In a saucepan over medium-low heat, melt the butter. Add the jalapeño (if using) and cook, stirring, for 1 minute. Sprinkle the flour over the top and whisk until smooth, letting it bubble for 1 minute.

Slowly add the milk and then the beer, whisking constantly, until the mixture is smooth, thick, and starts to bubble, about 2 minutes. Add the cheddar in small handfuls, stirring gently until each addition is melted. Add the American cheese a little at a time, stirring until the mixture is smooth. The mixture will be thick, but you can add more beer to get to the consistency you like.

Transfer to a bowl and serve with the chips or pretzels (or whatever you like!).

GILES: "You never train with me anymore. He's going to kick your ass."

BUFFY: "Giles!"

GILES: "Sorry. Was that a bit honest?"

"THE YOKO FACTOR" (SEASON 4, EPISODE 20)

MAKES 4 SERVINGS

Raw Power Beef Carpaccio

Raw and packed with primal flair, this beef carpaccio alludes to one of Sunnydale's earliest unsettling food moments, when Xander gets possessed by a hyena spirit and acquires a taste for raw meat. After a zoo trip goes wrong, Xander and a pack of students embrace their new predatory instincts, starting with lunch (RIP Herbert). Unlike that disturbing snack, this dish is refined and hauntingly good, layering tender, paper-thin slices of filet mignon with peppery arugula, briny capers, and a sharp vinaigrette.

Ingredients

8 ounces filet mignon

2 tablespoons extra-virgin olive oil

2 tablespoons canola oil

2 tablespoons red wine vinegar

1 teaspoon Dijon mustard

1 teaspoon honey

Pinch kosher salt, plus more for seasoning

Pinch freshly ground black pepper, plus more for seasoning

1 cup baby arugula

1 tablespoon capers, drained

Wrap the beef tightly in plastic wrap to create as round a shape as possible. Place in the freezer for 1 hour to partially freeze (this makes slicing much easier).

Meanwhile, make the vinaigrette: In a small jar with a lid, combine the olive oil, canola oil, vinegar, mustard, honey, salt, and pepper. Cover and shake vigorously until well combined. Set aside.

Using a very sharp knife, slice the tenderloin across the grain into ⅛-inch-thick slices. One at a time, place a slice of the tenderloin between two sheets of plastic wrap and gently pound the meat with the flat side of a meat pounder until paper-thin. Arrange the slices on a platter and season lightly with salt and pepper.

Place the arugula in a large bowl and drizzle it with some of the vinaigrette. Arrange the dressed arugula over the beef slices and sprinkle with the capers. Drizzle with more vinaigrette and serve at once.

"LET'S DO LUNCH."

—XANDER
"THE PACK" (SEASON 1, EPISODE 6)

MAKES 4 TO 6 SERVINGS

Spellbound Nachos

When Sunnydale's adults get magically teen-ified by cursed candy, Ms. Barton goes from study hall sub to nacho-hunting party girl at the Bronze, much to Willow's confusion. This recipe is a tribute to chaotic nights, questionable supervision, and dangerously melty snacks. Add taco meat or swap in Beer-Spiked Cheese Dip (page 37) for extra bite. And skip the preshredded cheese—like Sunnydale adults under a spell, it just doesn't behave right.

Ingredients

1 bag (8 to 10 ounces) thick-cut tortilla chips

6 ounces cheddar cheese, grated

6 ounces Monterey Jack cheese, grated

One 15-ounce can black beans, drained and rinsed

¼ cup chopped green onion, white and green parts

⅓ cup drained sliced pickled jalapeños

½ cup pico de gallo or your favorite salsa

½ cup prepared guacamole

½ cup sour cream

Position a rack in the upper third of the oven and preheat the oven to 350°F. Arrange the chips in an even layer on a large-rimmed baking sheet. Bake the chips for 5 minutes.

In a medium bowl, toss together the two cheeses. Sprinkle two-thirds of the cheese over the hot chips, making sure to cover them all evenly. Top evenly with the beans, the remaining cheese, the green onions, and jalapeños. Bake until the cheese is melted and the nachos are browned, 10 to 12 minutes. (If you like, at the end, turn on the broiler to brown the cheese a little more.)

Immediately top with the pico de gallo and dollops of the guacamole and sour cream, then serve at once, straight from the hot baking sheet.

"WILLOW . . . THAT'S A TREE. ARE THERE ANY NACHOS IN HERE, LITTLE TREE?"

—MS. BARTON

"BAND CANDY" (SEASON 3, EPISODE 6)

MAKES 6 SERVINGS

Hellmouth Jalapeño Poppers

Stuffed with molten cheese and crispy bacon, these fiery jalapeño poppers capture the heat and chaos of the Hellmouth. Like the portal beneath Sunnydale, they may look harmless at first, but one bite unleashes a rush of danger and flavor. Just as the Hellmouth draws supernatural forces from every corner, these poppers tend to draw a crowd and vanish quickly at any gathering.

Ingredients

2 thick slices smoked bacon (about 3 ounces total), chopped

¼ cup fine dried breadcrumbs

½ cup grated Parmesan cheese, divided

¼ teaspoon smoked paprika, plus more for garnish

8 ounces cream cheese, at room temperature

½ packed cup shredded cheddar or Jack cheese, or a mixture

1 green onion, white and green parts, finely chopped

12 medium jalapeños

In a frying pan over medium heat, cook the bacon, stirring occasionally, until crisp, about 8 minutes. Using a slotted spoon, transfer the bacon to paper towels.

In a medium bowl, stir together the breadcrumbs, ¼ cup of the Parmesan, and the paprika. In another bowl, stir together the cream cheese, cheddar, the remaining ¼ cup Parmesan, most of the bacon (save a little for garnish), and the green onion until well combined.

Position one rack in the upper third of the oven and another rack in the middle of the oven and preheat the oven to 400°F.

Wearing disposable gloves, halve the jalapeños lengthwise, then use a small spoon to scoop out and discard the seeds. Arrange the jalapeño halves, cut sides up, on a baking sheet.

Fill each jalapeño half with the cream cheese mixture, dividing it evenly. Press the cheesy side of the jalapeño into the breadcrumb mixture, pressing the crumbs to attach, then return to the baking sheet crumb-side up. Press a little bacon into the tops of the cheese to garnish.

Bake on the middle rack until bubbling and golden brown, about 15 minutes. Then turn on the broiler and move the baking sheet to the upper rack. Broil until nicely browned, about 2 minutes. (If any of the filling slides out, simply coax it back in with a spoon.) Let cool for about 5 minutes, then serve warm.

"WELL, THE HELLMOUTH, THE CENTER OF MYSTICAL CONVERGENCE, SUPERNATURAL MONSTERS: been there."

—XANDER
"NIGHTMARES" (SEASON 1, EPISODE 10)

MAKES 8 SKEWERS

Cross-Training Chicken Skewers

You may not be able to dust a vamp with the wooden stakes used in this recipe, but these grilled chicken skewers are packed with flavor and power, just right for a Slayer in training. Marinated in a zesty, gingery mixture and served with a rich peanut sauce, they're speared with wooden "stakes" (aka bamboo skewers), a nod to Buffy's preferred weapon. Tasty, portable, and full of protein, they're the ideal fuel for anyone juggling everyday life and supernatural battles.

Ingredients

1/3 cup well-shaken coconut milk

1 medium shallot, finely chopped

2 garlic cloves, finely chopped

2 packed tablespoons light brown sugar

2 tablespoons fish sauce

2 tablespoons freshly squeezed lime juice

2 teaspoons shredded fresh ginger

1 to 2 teaspoons sriracha, depending on how spicy you like it

1 teaspoon ground turmeric

Pinch kosher salt

Pinch freshly ground black pepper

1½ pounds boneless, skinless chicken thighs, trimmed and cut into 1-inch pieces or strips

Oil, for brushing

Peanut sauce, for serving

Special Equipment

Blender

Eight 8-inch bamboo skewers

Charcoal or gas grill

In a blender, combine the coconut milk, shallot, garlic, brown sugar, fish sauce, lime juice, ginger, sriracha, turmeric, salt, and pepper. Blend to a smooth purée.

Put the chicken pieces in a large bowl, pour the marinade over them, and toss gently to combine. Cover and refrigerate for 30 minutes or up to 4 hours.

Meanwhile, soak eight 8-inch bamboo skewers in water for 30 minutes.

Line a baking sheet with parchment paper. Thread the chicken onto the skewers, letting the excess marinade drip off and dividing the chicken evenly. Place the skewers on the prepared baking sheet.

Prepare a gas or charcoal grill for direct grilling over medium-high heat (about 550°F). Brush the grill grate with oil. Cook the skewers for 5 minutes on one side, until you see grill marks and the chicken releases from the grill. Turn and cook until nicely browned and cooked through, about 4 minutes longer.

Serve with the peanut sauce alongside for dipping.

"THERE IS ONLY ONE THING ON THIS EARTH MORE POWERFUL THAN EVIL, AND THAT'S US."

—BUFFY

"BRING ON THE NIGHT" (SEASON 7, EPISODE 10)

MAKES 16 CROSTINI (6 TO 8 SERVINGS)

Vampire Bite Crostini

Creamy white bean purée, roasted garlic, and a bold streak of sun-dried tomato create a bite-size tribute to the eternal dance between Slayer and vampire. A balsamic drizzle adds the final mark—sharp and darkly dramatic, like a fresh set of fangs. Inspired by the tension and allure of Sunnydale's undead nightlife, these crostini are equal parts elegance and edge.

Ingredients

1 garlic head, plus 2 peeled cloves for rubbing

3 tablespoons extra-virgin olive oil, divided, plus more for brushing

½ teaspoon kosher salt, plus more for seasoning

1 baguette, cut crosswise into sixteen ⅓-inch-thick slices

¼ teaspoon freshly ground black pepper, plus more for seasoning

One 15-ounce can white beans, such as cannellini or great northern, drained and rinsed

2 tablespoons drained and finely chopped sun-dried tomatoes in oil

1 tablespoon freshly squeezed lemon juice

1 teaspoon minced fresh rosemary

Balsamic vinegar, for drizzling

Chopped fresh basil, for serving

Special Equipment

Blender

Preheat the oven to 400°F.

Slice off the top of the head of garlic. Place the garlic cut side up on a piece of aluminum foil. Drizzle with 1 tablespoon of the olive oil and then sprinkle with a pinch of salt. Wrap the garlic tightly in the foil and roast for about 40 minutes or until the cloves are golden brown and very tender. Set aside until cool enough to handle.

While the garlic is roasting, make the crostini. Brush both sides of the baguette slices lightly with oil and season lightly with salt and pepper. Bake until crisp and golden brown, turning once, about 10 minutes. Set aside.

Squeeze the roasted garlic cloves into a blender, discarding the skins. Add the beans, the remaining 2 tablespoons olive oil, the sun-dried tomatoes, lemon juice, rosemary, ½ teaspoon salt, and ¼ teaspoon pepper. Blend to a smooth purée. Taste and season with more salt and pepper if needed. Scrape into a bowl and set aside.

Arrange the crostini on a platter and lightly rub the top of each slice with the peeled (uncooked) garlic cloves. Spread each piece of toast with the white bean mixture. Drizzle the crostini with balsamic vinegar and sprinkle with basil. Serve at once.

"I DIDN'T SAY I'D NEVER SLAY ANOTHER VAMPIRE. IT'S NOT LIKE I HAVE ALL THESE FLUFFY BUNNY FEELINGS FOR THEM. I'M JUST NOT GOING TO GET WAY EXTRACURRICULAR WITH IT."

—BUFFY
"WELCOME TO THE HELLMOUTH"
(SEASON 1, EPISODE 1)

MAKES 4 SERVINGS

Bite Me Blossom

This blooming fried onion is a crunchy, golden tribute to one of Spike's most unexpected soft spots. While riding through Sunnydale with Andrew, he admits, "Not as good as those onion blossom things . . . It's an onion and it's a flower." Andrew marvels at the concept, and Spike explains the genius behind the crisp petals. It's a rare moment of bonding—proof that even the toughest vampires have a weakness for deep-fried brilliance. Like friendship, it's not the easiest thing to make, but it's always worth it.

Ingredients

1 large sweet white onion

1 cup whole milk

1 large egg

1½ teaspoons kosher salt, divided, plus more for seasoning

1 cup all-purpose flour

1 teaspoon garlic powder

1 teaspoon dried oregano

½ teaspoon freshly ground black pepper

Canola oil, for deep-frying

Mystery Sauce (page 80), garlic aioli, or other favorite dipping sauce, for serving

Special Equipment

Deep-fry thermometer

"TELL ANYONE WE HAD THIS CONVERSATION, I'LL BITE YOU."

—SPIKE
"EMPTY PLACES"
(SEASON 7, EPISODE 19)

Trim off the top ½ inch of the onion and peel away and discard the skin. Using a very sharp chef's knife, quarter the onion lengthwise from the top to the root end, stopping the cut about ½ inch from the root end. It's important not to cut all the way through so the onion stays intact. Slice each quarter lengthwise into 4 sections, again stopping the cut about ½ inch from the root end; you should have 16 sections total. Turn the onion root side up and check to make sure the cuts go nearly to the root end.

Fill a large bowl with ice water and gently submerge the onion root end up in the water. Set aside to soak for 30 to 60 minutes (this helps the onion "bloom").

Remove the onion from the water, letting all the water drip away. Set the onion root side up on paper towels to drain completely.

In a medium bowl, whisk together the milk and egg with ½ teaspoon of the salt. In another medium bowl, whisk together the flour, garlic powder, dried oregano, the remaining 1 teaspoon salt, and the pepper.

Place the onion root side down in a large empty bowl. Spread the "petals" apart. Sprinkle half of the seasoned flour mixture all over the onion, making sure to completely coat it. Carefully turn the onion upside down and gently shake away the excess flour.

Dunk the onion into the egg mixture, completely coating the onion. Remove the onion, letting the excess egg mixture drip off, then repeat the flouring process, gently shaking off any excess flour from the onion. Place the onion root, side down, on a plate and refrigerate while you heat the oil.

Fill a large, deep saucepan with at least 3 inches of oil, making sure the pot is no more than half full so you have plenty of space at the top and the sides. Heat the oil over medium-high heat until a deep-fry thermometer registers 365°F.

Using a wire skimmer or a spider, carefully lower the onion, root side up, into the hot oil. Adjust the heat immediately so the oil temperature stays near 350°F.

Fry until the onion turns light golden brown, 4 to 5 minutes, then very carefully turn the onion and cook until golden brown, about 3 minutes longer. Drain on paper towels, then transfer to a plate, cut side up. Season with salt and serve with the Mystery Sauce on the side, for dipping.

MONDAY

SWEET LIVE @ 9PM

TUESDAY

WORLD CULTURE DANCE @ 7PM

WEDNESDAY

DINGOES ATE MY BABY LIVE @ 9PM

THURSDAY

SHY LIVE ON STAGE @ 9PM

FRIDAY

ANNUAL FUMIGATION PARTY! @ 8PM
CATCH A ROACH, GET A FREE DRINK!

SATURDAY

SUNNYDALE HIGH HOMECOMING @ 7PM

SUNDAY

JONATHAN LIVE @ 8PM

MAKES 4 SERVINGS

Potential Pakoras

These crispy cauliflower bites are seasoned with ginger, garam masala, and chili powder, then dipped in chickpea flour batter and fried until golden. Cooling yogurt or cilantro chutney provides the perfect balance of flavor. With their hidden burst of spice, these pakoras mirror the strength of the Potential Slayers—young women like Dawn, who unexpectedly becomes a Slayer when Willow's locator spell surrounds her with a glowing aura. As Dawn faces her new destiny and worries for Buffy's safety, the Potentials' true power begins to rise against the looming threat of the First Evil.

Ingredients

1 teaspoon garam masala

½ teaspoon chili powder

½ teaspoon ground ginger

¼ teaspoon garlic powder

1 teaspoon kosher salt, divided, plus more for seasoning

12 ounces cauliflower florets, cut into 1½ inch pieces

½ cup chickpea flour (gram flour)

¼ cup white rice flour

2 tablespoons cornstarch

½ cup water, plus more as needed

Canola oil, for deep-frying

Lemon wedges, for serving

Green chutney (such as cilantro), tamarind chutney, or yogurt, for serving

Special Equipment

Deep-fry thermometer

In a medium bowl, stir together the garam masala, chili powder, ginger, garlic powder, and ½ teaspoon of the salt. Add the cauliflower and toss to coat.

In another medium bowl, whisk together the chickpea flour, rice flour, cornstarch, and the remaining ½ teaspoon salt. Stir in the water and whisk to combine. Add more water if needed, by the tablespoonful, to make a batter that is just thick enough to coat the cauliflower but not too thick.

Fill a large saucepan over medium-high heat with 2 inches of oil and heat to 350°F on a deep-fry thermometer.

In three or four batches, dip the seasoned florets in the batter, letting any excess drip off. Then carefully add the cauliflower to the hot oil. Do not overcrowd the pot. Fry, stirring and turning often, until crisp, tender, and golden brown, 3 to 4 minutes.

Using a slotted spoon or a spider, transfer the fried cauliflower to paper towels to drain. Sprinkle with a little salt. Repeat with the remaining cauliflower. Serve hot, with the lemon wedges and chutney alongside for dipping.

"AND THE LIGHT WILL FIND THE POTENTIAL, AND IT WILL ILLUMINATE HER WITH A GLOWING AURA."

—WILLOW

"POTENTIAL" (SEASON 7, EPISODE 12)

CHAPTER THREE

"LET'S DO LUNCH"

"THIS BIG EVIL THAT'S BEEN PROMISING TO DEVOUR US? WELL, I THINK IT'S STARTED CHOMPING."

—WILLOW

"NEVER LEAVE ME" (SEASON 7, EPISODE 9)

When you're living on a Hellmouth, getting eaten is always on the table, so maybe it's time you bite back. From Slayer-size sandwiches to soul-saving soups and salads, this chapter is packed with midday meals to keep you strong, snarky, and ready for whatever the apocalypse serves up next.

MAKES 6 SERVINGS

Roasted "Babies" Carrot Salad with Citrus-Ale Vinaigrette

This vibrant salad takes a mischievous cue from one of Anya's magical misfires. When she and Willow clash over a spell, their bickering accidentally summons Olaf the troll—a beer-loving brute with a taste for destruction and a disturbing craving for "plump, succulent babies." Oops! These roasted "baby" carrots offer a far more appetizing option, nestled among arugula, tangy goat cheese, and pistachios, all dressed in a bright citrus-ale vinaigrette. Chaotic origin, delicious result.

Ingredients

Vinaigrette

¼ cup extra-virgin olive oil

2 tablespoons white wine vinegar

1 tablespoon ale or freshly squeezed orange juice

2 teaspoons whole-grain mustard

1 teaspoon minced shallot

1 teaspoon finely grated orange zest

1 teaspoon honey

Pinch kosher salt

Pinch freshly ground black pepper

Salad

1 pound baby carrots

1 tablespoon extra-virgin olive oil

1 teaspoon honey

Kosher salt

Freshly ground black pepper

8 cups baby arugula (about 8 ounces)

½ cup crumbled fresh goat cheese (about 4 ounces)

¼ cup roughly chopped roasted pistachios (shelled)

Crostini (see page 47), for serving

TO MAKE THE VINAIGRETTE: Put the olive oil, vinegar, ale, mustard, shallot, orange zest, honey, a pinch of salt, and a pinch of pepper into a jar that has a tight-fitting lid. Close the lid and shake the jar vigorously until the dressing is completely emulsified. Set aside.

TO MAKE THE SALAD: Preheat the oven to 450°F. On a baking sheet, toss the carrots with the oil, honey, a pinch of salt, and several grinds of pepper. Spread in a single layer. Roast until nicely browned, crisp, and tender, stirring once or twice, about 15 minutes. Set aside to cool slightly, then halve or quarter depending on the size.

Place the arugula and carrots in a large bowl and drizzle with a little vinaigrette, then season with salt and pepper. Toss to coat. Transfer to a platter or individual plates. Garnish with the goat cheese and pistachios, and serve with crostini alongside, plus more vinaigrette.

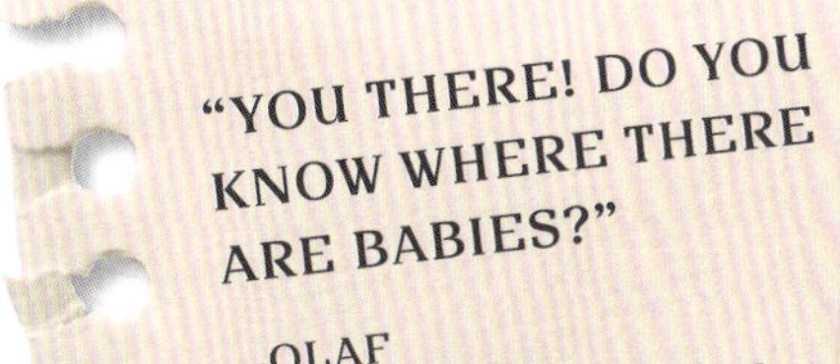

MAKES 6 SERVINGS

GRILLED "STAKE" SALAD

This grilled steak salad honors the beloved Mr. Pointy, Buffy's iconic wooden stake. Given to her by fellow Slayer Kendra, Mr. Pointy becomes a trusted weapon and symbol of strength throughout Buffy's vamp hunts. Buffy keeps it close, even imagining bronzing it someday. With fresh herbs, crisp veggies, and a tangy lime–garlic dressing, this salad is a bold, flavorful tribute to the Slayer's fierce fight and her legendary weapon.

INGREDIENTS

MARINADE/DRESSING

¼ cup canola or avocado oil

¼ cup roughly chopped fresh cilantro, including tender stems

2 garlic cloves, chopped

1 red Fresno chile, halved, seeded, and chopped

2 tablespoons fish sauce

2 packed tablespoons light brown sugar

3 tablespoons freshly squeezed lime juice

¼ teaspoon kosher salt

STEAK AND SALAD

1½ pounds boneless beef chuck roast, trimmed of excess fat and cut into 1-inch pieces

1 teaspoon kosher salt

1 small red onion, cut into 1½-inch pieces

Canola oil, for brushing

8 cups mixed baby lettuces or chopped hearts of romaine

½ cup halved cherry tomatoes

½ English cucumber, halved lengthwise, seeded, and cut into thin crosswise slices, or 2 Persian cucumbers, thinly sliced

¼ cup roughly chopped fresh cilantro, plus more for garnish

¼ cup roughly chopped fresh mint leaves, plus more for garnish

⅓ cup chopped roasted peanuts

SPECIAL EQUIPMENT

Blender

6 metal or bamboo skewers

Charcoal or gas grill

TO MAKE THE MARINADE/DRESSING: Combine the oil, cilantro, garlic, chile, fish sauce, brown sugar, lime juice, and salt in a blender and blend until smooth.

TO MAKE THE STEAK AND SALAD: Put the meat into a medium bowl, sprinkle with the salt, and toss to coat. Pour ¼ cup of the marinade over the meat and toss to coat evenly. Cover and refrigerate for at least 2 hours or up to 8 hours. (If using bamboo skewers, soak them in water for at least 30 minutes.)

Prepare a charcoal or gas grill for direct-heat cooking over medium-high heat (425°F). Brush the grill grates clean.

While the grill is heating, prepare the kebabs. Thread the steak and onion pieces onto 6 metal or soaked bamboo skewers. Brush with a little oil.

Grill the kebabs over direct heat, turning them a few times, until evenly charred and the steak is done to your liking, about 8 minutes for medium-rare or 10 minutes for medium. Transfer the kebabs to a platter and let them rest while you make the salad.

In a large bowl, toss together the lettuce, cherry tomatoes, cucumber, cilantro, and mint. Drizzle with some of the remaining dressing, tossing to coat. Divide among 6 plates, top each with a steak kebab, and garnish with peanuts, cilantro, and mint. Serve with any remaining dressing alongside.

"IN CASE THE CURSE DOES NOT SUCCEED, THIS IS MY LUCKY STAKE. I'VE KILLED MANY VAMPIRES WITH IT. I CALL IT MR. POINTY."

—KENDRA
"BECOMING, PART 1"
(SEASON 2, EPISODE 21)

SUNNYDALE SHS HIGH

CLASS CLOWN
XANDER

FAVORITE TEACHER
GILES

FUTURE NOBEL PRIZE WINNER
WILLOW

MOST CHANGED
OZ

MOST POPULAR
CORDELIA

CLASS PROTECTOR
BUFFY

MAKES 4 SERVINGS

Five-by-Five Salad

Slaying stirs up an appetite, and no one embraces that truth like Faith. This protein-packed salad could easily be her go-to post-dust snack: hearty grilled chicken, creamy avocado, sharp cheddar, and hard-boiled eggs, all drenched in a punchy homemade ranch dressing. It's bold, messy, and a little extra, just like Faith. Perfect for when you're starving *and* feeling dangerous.

Ingredients

Ranch Dressing

¼ cup buttermilk

1 teaspoon freshly squeezed lemon juice

1 teaspoon each minced fresh dill, chives, and flat-leaf parsley

½ teaspoon onion powder

¼ teaspoon garlic powder

¼ teaspoon freshly ground black pepper

½ cup mayonnaise

Pinch kosher salt (optional)

Grilled Chicken and Salad

1 pound boneless, skinless chicken breasts

1 teaspoon fine sea salt

1 teaspoon freshly ground black pepper

6 cups mixed greens

¼ small red onion, very thinly sliced

½ English cucumber, halved lengthwise and cut into thin crosswise slices

1 cup halved cherry tomatoes

1 large ripe avocado, halved, pitted, peeled, and cubed

½ cup shredded cheddar, crumbled blue cheese, or crumbled feta

4 hard-boiled eggs, peeled and quartered lengthwise

Special Equipment

Charcoal or gas grill

TO MAKE THE RANCH DRESSING: In a medium bowl, whisk together the buttermilk, lemon juice, herbs, onion powder, garlic powder, and pepper until blended. Stir in the mayonnaise. Taste and season with salt, if needed.

TO MAKE THE GRILLED CHICKEN AND SALAD: Using a meat mallet, lightly pound each chicken breast to an even thickness (¾ to 1 inch). Season the chicken all over with salt and pepper, place into a shallow baking dish, and spread with ¼ cup of the ranch dressing. Refrigerate for at least 30 minutes or up to 2 hours.

Preheat a charcoal or gas grill for direct grilling over medium heat (about 400°F). Brush the grill grates clean. Grill the chicken, with the lid closed, until it releases easily from the grates, about 4 minutes. Turn and grill the other side until opaque all the way through, about 5 minutes. Set aside to rest for at least 10 minutes. Chop the chicken into bite-size pieces.

In a large, wide bowl, toss together the greens, onion, cucumber, and cherry tomatoes. Add the chopped chicken and ¼ cup of the ranch dressing and toss to coat evenly. Transfer to a serving platter. Sprinkle the avocado and cheese over the top and arrange the egg wedges around the salad. Serve with the remaining dressing alongside.

"GOD, I COULD EAT A HORSE. ISN'T IT CRAZY HOW SLAYIN' JUST ALWAYS MAKES YOU HUNGRY AND HORNY?"

—FAITH
"FAITH, HOPE & TRICK"
(SEASON 3, EPISODE 3)

and darkness, her
and the sword.
before the

MAKES 4 SERVINGS

Apocalyptic Avocado Toast

In Sunnydale, the apocalypse is always just around the corner, whether it's the Hellmouth rumbling under your feet or some ancient evil trying to end the world. Even a Slayer needs a lunch break. This is total end-of-the-world snackage: creamy, crunchy, and deceptively chill. Like Buffy herself, it balances light and dark, power and poise. One bite and *boom*, you're five by five and ready to save the world. Again.

Ingredients

Tahini-Miso Dressing

3 tablespoons tahini

2 tablespoons freshly squeezed lemon juice

1 tablespoon white miso

2 tablespoons extra-virgin olive oil

2 tablespoons water, plus more as needed

Avocado Toasts

2 tablespoons canola oil

½ cup cooked chickpeas, rinsed, drained, and patted dry

¼ teaspoon kosher salt, plus more for seasoning

4 large, thick slices artisan bread

2 large ripe avocados, halved, pitted, peeled, and thinly sliced

¼ teaspoon freshly ground black pepper

1 teaspoon black sesame seeds

TO MAKE THE TAHINI-MISO DRESSING: Put the tahini, lemon juice, and miso into a small jar with a tight-fitting lid. Using a fork, whip together the ingredients until smooth. Add the oil and water. Close the jar and shake vigorously. Thin with a little more water, if necessary, to make a dressing with a pourable consistency. Set aside.

TO MAKE THE AVOCADO TOASTS: In a frying pan over medium heat, warm the oil. Pat the chickpeas dry, then add them to the hot oil. Cook, stirring occasionally, until crisp and golden brown, 2 to 3 minutes. Transfer to a plate lined with paper towels and season with salt.

Toast the bread in a toaster or under the broiler. Fan out ½ an avocado on top of each piece of toast. Using a fork, gently smash the avocado into the toast. Season with salt and pepper. Drizzle the tahini-miso dressing over the avocado, sprinkle the toasted chickpeas and sesame seeds on top, and serve at once.

"IF THE APOCALYPSE COMES, BEEP ME."

—BUFFY "NEVER KILL A BOY ON THE FIRST DATE" (SEASON 1, EPISODE 5)

MAKES 4 SANDWICHES

Cheese Man Melt

This grilled cheese, layered with sweet, caramelized onions and pressed between buttery garlic bread, channels the surreal, dream-soaked night when Buffy and her friends crash after defeating Season 4 antagonist Adam. As Buffy, Willow, Xander, and Giles each confront their hidden fears and desires in "Restless," one absurd constant ties them together: the mysterious Cheese Man popping up with slices of cheese and no explanation. As Buffy says, "I think I speak for everyone here when I say 'huh?'"

Ingredients

7 tablespoons salted butter, at room temperature, divided

1 teaspoon Italian seasoning

¾ teaspoon garlic powder

1 yellow onion, halved and thinly sliced

Pinch kosher salt

8 slices artisan bread

5 ounces Gruyère cheese, shredded

4 ounces low-moisture mozzarella cheese, shredded

In a small bowl, combine 6 tablespoons of the butter with the Italian seasoning and garlic powder.

In a frying pan over medium-low heat, melt the remaining 1 tablespoon butter. Add the onion and salt and cook, stirring occasionally, until golden brown and tender, about 9 minutes. Transfer to a plate.

To assemble the sandwiches, lay out the bread slices on a countertop. Top 4 of the slices with half the Gruyère and mozzarella, dividing it evenly among the slices. Top each cheese-topped bread slice with a quarter of the onions, in an even layer. Top the onions with the remaining cheese, dividing it evenly among the slices. Top with the remaining bread slices.

Spread the top of each sandwich with some of the garlic-herb butter, using half of it.

Heat a large griddle or frying pan (or 2 frying pans) over medium heat. Add the sandwiches, buttered sides down. Spread the remaining butter over the unbuttered tops of the sandwiches. Cook until the bottoms of the sandwiches are golden brown, about 4 minutes, then carefully turn the sandwiches. Press down on the sandwiches with your spatula to help them stick together, and continue to cook until the cheese is melted and the bread is golden brown and toasted to your liking, about 3 minutes longer.

Transfer to plates, cut in half if you'd like, and serve.

"I WEAR THE CHEESE. IT DOES NOT WEAR ME."

—THE CHEESE MAN, "RESTLESS" (SEASON 4, EPISODE 22)

MAKES 4 SANDWICHES

Hellmouth High Sloppy Joes

A little spicy, a little messy—just like high school, especially when the high school sits atop the Hellmouth portal to other dimensions. This chipotle-kicked sloppy joe with melted cheddar and pickled jalapeños is a nod to Buffy's early Sunnydale High days, when crushes and bullies collided, making for some serious cafeteria drama. Never forget when Cordelia tries to go to Dateville with Owen by sending Buffy's lunch tray crashing to the ground. Luckily, Owen isn't impressed and instead shuns the self-proclaimed slayer of dating in favor of the true Slayer.

Ingredients

- 1 tablespoon canola oil
- ½ yellow onion, finely chopped
- 1 celery stalk, diced
- ¼ cup finely diced green bell pepper
- ¼ cup finely diced red bell pepper
- ¾ teaspoon kosher salt, divided
- 1 pound lean ground beef
- One 8-ounce can tomato sauce
- 1/3 cup ketchup
- 1 chipotle chile in adobo sauce, minced, plus 2 teaspoons adobo sauce
- 1 tablespoon country Dijon mustard
- 1 tablespoon apple cider vinegar
- 1 packed tablespoon light brown sugar
- 2 teaspoons Worcestershire sauce
- 1 teaspoon chili powder
- ½ teaspoon granulated garlic
- ¼ teaspoon freshly ground black pepper
- 4 burger buns, split
- 4 sandwich-size slices cheddar cheese or American cheese
- ¼ cup sliced pickled jalapeños

In a large saucepan over medium heat, warm the oil. Add the onion, celery, bell peppers, and ¼ teaspoon of the salt and cook, stirring occasionally, until the vegetables are tender and begin to brown, about 5 minutes. Add the beef, increase the heat to medium-high and cook, stirring and breaking up the beef, until it is no longer pink, about 4 minutes.

Stir in the tomato sauce, ketchup, chipotle chile and adobo sauce, mustard, vinegar, brown sugar, Worcestershire sauce, chili powder, garlic, pepper, and the remaining ½ teaspoon salt. Bring the mixture to a simmer. Reduce the heat to low and cook, stirring occasionally, until thickened, about 25 minutes.

Toast the buns. Place the bottom halves of the buns, cut sides up, on individual plates and top with the beef mixture, dividing it equally. Top each with cheddar and pickled jalapeños. Cover with the bun tops and serve right away.

"AT LEAST YOU DON'T HAVE TO EAT YOUR SOYLENT GREEN."

—OWEN

"NEVER KILL A BOY ON THE FIRST DATE" (SEASON 1, EPISODE 5)

MAKES 4 SANDWICHES

Caveman Turkey-Bacon Sandwich with Slayer Slaw

Buffy love sandwich . . . During a lecture in "Beer Bad," Willow watches Buffy casually reach over and snag a classmate's sandwich mid-sentence, taking a huge bite. Turns out, someone spiked the beer at the Bronze, turning Buffy and a group of upperclassmen into cavemen with some übersucky manners. Stacked with smoked turkey, crispy bacon, sharp cheddar, and a crunchy, tangy apple-cabbage slaw, it will satisfy even your most primal desire. Not into slaw? Sub in thick tomato slices, lettuce, or creamy avocado.

Ingredients

Slaw

¼ cup mayonnaise

2 tablespoons rice vinegar

1 teaspoon sugar (optional)

Kosher salt

Freshly ground black pepper

2 packed cups finely shredded green cabbage

1 small Granny Smith apple, cored and grated

1 tablespoon finely chopped red onion

Sandwiches

8 slices thick-cut bacon

4 large sandwich rolls, such as ciabatta or whole wheat, split and toasted

½ cup garlic aioli

12 ounces sliced smoked turkey

4 to 8 sandwich-size slices sharp cheddar cheese

TO MAKE THE SLAW: In a medium bowl, whisk together the mayonnaise, vinegar, and sugar (if using). Season with salt and pepper to taste. Add the cabbage, apple, and onion and toss to coat. Cover and refrigerate until chilled, about 30 minutes or up to 2 hours.

TO MAKE THE SANDWICHES: In a frying pan over medium-low heat, cook the bacon, turning once or twice, until the fat renders and the bacon becomes crispy, about 8 minutes. Transfer to paper towels to drain.

Spread the cut sides of the rolls with the garlic aioli. Top the bottom halves of the rolls with the turkey, cheese, and bacon, dividing them among the rolls and layering them evenly. Top each with some slaw. Cap each sandwich with a roll top. Cut each sandwich in half and serve at once.

"I'M SUFFERING THE AFTERNESS OF A BAD NIGHT OF BADNESS."

—BUFFY
"BEER BAD" (SEASON 4, EPISODE 5)

MAKES 4 SERVINGS

Bloody Tomato Mug Soup

Spike's not exactly living his best undead life—chained up in Giles's bathtub, sipping warm pig's blood from a mug while Buffy grills him for information that he refuses to give. Willow proposes a truth spell, but grief over Oz sends her down a darker path, leading to magical chaos: Buffy falls for Spike, Giles goes blind, and Xander attracts demons. This Bloody Tomato Mug Soup honors that iconic scene with a creamy tomato-herb soup served in a mug with garlic croutons. Want a kick? Add cayenne or red pepper flakes.

Ingredients

2 tablespoons extra-virgin olive oil

½ yellow onion, finely chopped

1½ teaspoons kosher salt, divided

2 garlic cloves, minced

One 28-ounce can crushed tomatoes

One 12-ounce jar roasted red peppers, drained and chopped

1 teaspoon Italian seasoning

½ teaspoon freshly ground black pepper, plus more for seasoning

⅓ cup heavy cream

Crostini, rubbed with a garlic clove (see page 47), for serving

Special Equipment

Blender or immersion blender

In a saucepan over medium heat, warm the oil. Add the onion and ¼ teaspoon of the salt and cook, stirring, until the onion is soft, about 6 minutes. Add the garlic and cook until fragrant, about 1 minute.

Add the tomatoes, peppers, Italian seasoning, 1 teaspoon of the salt, and the pepper and stir to combine. Bring to a simmer and then reduce the heat to low and cook, stirring, until the flavors come together, about 10 minutes. Transfer the mixture to a blender (or use an immersion blender in the pot) and purée until smooth. If using a blender, return the soup to the saucepan.

Stir in the cream, then warm the soup over low heat. Taste and season with the remaining ¼ teaspoon salt and pepper if needed. Ladle into mugs or bowls and serve with the garlic-rubbed crostini on the side.

"COMFY? I'M CHAINED IN A BATHTUB, DRINKING PIG'S BLOOD FROM A NOVELTY MUG. DOESN'T RATE HUGE IN THE ZAGAT'S GUIDE."

—SPIKE
"SOMETHING BLUE" (SEASON 4, EPISODE 9)

MAKES 4 TO 6 SERVINGS

Soulless Tortilla Soup

After a night of passion with Buffy, Angel loses his soul and becomes Angelus, the ruthless vampire who joins forces with Spike, Drusilla, and the demon Judge to hunt her down. When the person you trusted turns cold and dangerous overnight, you need something spicy and grounding in order to keep slaying. This tortilla soup is hot, messy, and full of bite—the kind of comfort that helps you hold it together when everything falls apart.

Ingredients

Soup

1 tablespoon canola oil

½ yellow onion, sliced

1 teaspoon kosher salt, divided

1 jalapeño, seeded and chopped

3 garlic cloves, roughly chopped

1 teaspoon ground cumin

1 teaspoon chili powder

One 14-ounce can diced tomatoes with juices

2 cups chicken stock, plus more as needed

One 15-ounce can black beans, drained and rinsed

¼ teaspoon freshly ground black pepper

2 cups shredded cooked chicken

½ cup fresh (or thawed frozen) corn kernels

Juice of 1 lime, plus wedges for serving

¼ cup chopped fresh cilantro

Toppings

Tortilla chips, broken into pieces

Cubed avocado

Sliced radishes

Cotija cheese

Special Equipment

Blender

TO MAKE THE SOUP: In a large saucepan over medium heat, warm the oil. Add the onion, season with ½ teaspoon of the salt, and cook, stirring, until well browned, about 5 minutes. Stir in the jalapeño, garlic, cumin, and chili powder until fragrant, about 1 minute.

Transfer the mixture to a blender. Add the tomatoes and chicken stock and blend until puréed.

Pour the mixture back into the saucepan and bring to a simmer over medium heat. Add the beans and season with the remaining ½ teaspoon salt and the pepper. Simmer for 10 minutes. Add the chicken, corn, and lime juice and simmer for 5 minutes or until the mixture is warmed through and the corn is tender.

Stir in the cilantro.

TO FINISH: Ladle the soup into bowls, sprinkle some tortilla chip pieces on top, and serve with the avocado, radish, and Cotija cheese on the side.

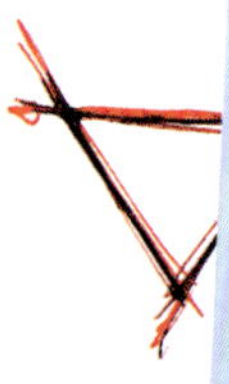

"IF ANGEL ACHIEVED TRUE HAPPINESS, EVEN JUST A MOMENT . . . HE WOULD LOSE HIS SOUL."

—JENNY CALENDAR
"INNOCENCE" (SEASON 2, EPISODE 14)

MAKES 4 SANDWICHES

Parmageddon

After a brutal battle with the godlike Glory, Buffy, Dawn, Willow, and Tara regroup and refuel by passing around their favorite sandwiches. Buffy's eggplant Parmesan sandwich, with tender, crunchy breadcrumb- and Parmesan-crusted eggplant, blood-red marinara, and melty mozzarella, is battle-ready comfort food. Dawn's surprising peanut butter and salami combo gives Buffy some major ew—but both sandwiches are exactly what they need to face whatever comes next.

Ingredients

Marinara Sauce

2 tablespoons extra-virgin olive oil

½ yellow onion, finely chopped

2 teaspoons Italian seasoning

1 teaspoon kosher salt

½ teaspoon freshly ground black pepper

One 28-ounce can crushed tomatoes

Baked Eggplant

1 Italian eggplant (about 1¼ pounds), cut into ⅓-inch-thick rounds (about 12 slices)

1¾ teaspoons kosher salt, divided

2 cups fresh breadcrumbs

½ cup grated Parmesan cheese, plus more for serving

½ teaspoon freshly ground black pepper, divided

½ cup all-purpose flour

2 large eggs

3 tablespoons extra-virgin olive oil, plus more if needed

TO MAKE THE MARINARA SAUCE: In a saucepan over medium heat, warm the oil. Add the onion and cook, stirring, until tender, about 5 minutes. Stir in the Italian seasoning, salt, and pepper, then add the crushed tomatoes. Bring to a boil, then reduce the heat to low and simmer, partially covered and stirring occasionally, until slightly thickened, about 30 minutes. Set aside. (The marinara can be cooled to room temperature, then stored in an airtight container in the refrigerator for up to 1 week.)

TO MAKE THE BAKED EGGPLANT: Lay the eggplant slices on a wire rack and sprinkle with 1½ teaspoons of the salt on both sides. Arrange in a single layer and set aside for 30 minutes. Using paper towels, blot the eggplant slices dry.

Place a rimmed baking sheet on the center rack of the oven and preheat the oven to 425°F.

In a shallow bowl, whisk together the breadcrumbs, Parmesan, the remaining ¼ teaspoon salt, and ¼ teaspoon of the pepper. In another shallow bowl, beat together the eggs. In a third bowl, combine the flour and the remaining ¼ teaspoon pepper. Toss the eggplant slices a few at a time in the flour, then dip each in the beaten egg, letting any excess egg drip off, then finally press into the breadcrumb mixture. Set aside on a clean baking sheet.

(Continued on page 71)

EP

Sandwiches

1 cup Marinara Sauce (page 69), warmed, plus more for dipping if you like

4 hoagie-style sandwich rolls, toasted

8 ounces low-moisture mozzarella, thinly sliced

Remove the heated baking sheet from the oven and drizzle it with the olive oil. Arrange the breaded eggplant on the baking sheet in a single layer. Bake until crisp and deeply golden, about 30 minutes, turning the eggplant slices halfway through cooking and drizzling with a little more oil if needed.

As soon as the eggplant is done, spread the cut sides of the toasted rolls with some warm marinara. Layer the eggplant and cheese on the rolls, top with more marinara to help melt the cheese, and serve at once.

CHAPTER FOUR

MONSTROUS MAINS

"WHY DON'T YOU HAVE DINNER AT OUR PLACE? MY MOM IS MAKING HER FAMOUS PHONE CALL TO THE CHINESE PLACE."

—XANDER

"OUT OF MIND, OUT OF SIGHT" (SEASON 1, EPISODE 11)

After a long night patrolling cemeteries or dodging demon goo, you've earned something more satisfying than a bag of chips. These hearty mains—think cheesy pizza, comforting noodles and pasta, and soul-warming stew—are perfect for refueling before your next run-in with the supernatural. Just remember: Keep the garlic bread close—you never know when it might come in handy.

MAKES 4 TO 6 SERVINGS

Double Trouble Sheet-Pan Pizza

Pizza is practically its own character in the Buffyverse—whether it's Xander delivering pies for Mr. Smith's Pizza Delivery or Ted creepily baking mini ones (page 36) for Buffy and the gang. This Double Trouble Sheet-Pan Pizza is a nod to those cheesy moments: double meat, double cheese, and all baked on a thick, golden crust. Even the Master would rise for a slice of this pie.

Ingredients

Pizza Dough

(Makes 2 pounds dough, enough for 1 large sheet-pan pizza)

1⅓ cups warm water (110°F)

1 tablespoon instant yeast

1 tablespoon sugar

3½ cups (1 pound 2 ounces) all-purpose flour, plus more as needed

2 teaspoons kosher salt

2 tablespoons extra-virgin olive oil, plus more for the bowl

Nonstick cooking spray

Sheet-Pan Pizza

1 pound Italian sausage, casings removed

Extra-virgin olive oil, for brushing

¾ cup Marinara Sauce (page 69) or your favorite pizza sauce

3 ounces sliced pepperoni

12 ounces low-moisture mozzarella cheese, shredded

¼ cup grated Parmesan cheese

¼ red onion, very thinly sliced

"SHALL I ORDER A PIZZA? DON'T TEENS IN A SNIT LIKE PIZZA?"

—XANDER
"HIM" (SEASON 7, EPISODE 6)

TO MAKE THE PIZZA DOUGH: In a medium bowl, whisk together the warm water, yeast, and sugar. Set aside for 10 minutes until foamy.

In a large bowl, stir together the flour and salt. Add the yeast mixture and olive oil to the flour mixture. Using a wooden spoon or your hands, stir the dough until well mixed. The dough should be soft and a bit sticky. Turn the dough out onto a floured work surface and, using floured hands, knead until soft, about 3 minutes. (Alternatively, make and knead the dough in a stand mixer using a dough hook.)

Clean out the large bowl and rub it with olive oil. Form the dough into a ball, transfer it to the oiled bowl, and cover the bowl loosely with a damp kitchen towel. Set aside in a warm, draft-free spot until the dough has doubled in size, about 1 hour.

Generously grease a 17-by-13-inch rimmed baking sheet with cooking spray. Transfer the dough to the baking sheet. Gently pull it out to fit the pan; if the dough springs back, let it rest for 5 minutes before continuing. Let the dough rise until slightly puffy, about 20 minutes.

While the dough rests, position a rack in the upper third of the oven and preheat the oven to 450°F. Par-bake the pizza crust for 8 minutes, then set aside.

TO MAKE THE SHEET-PAN PIZZA: Crumble the sausage into a frying pan over medium-high heat. Cook, stirring occasionally, until the sausage is browned and cooked through, about 6 minutes.

Brush the dough lightly with olive oil. Leaving a ½-inch border, spread the sauce over the dough. Top evenly with the sausage and pepperoni, then top with the mozzarella and Parmesan cheeses, and finally the red onion.

Bake the pizza on the upper rack until the crust is golden brown, about 18 minutes. Let cool for a few minutes, then slide the pizza off the baking sheet and onto a cutting board. Slice and serve right away.

MAKES 6 SERVINGS

Family Spaghetti Dinner

Family dinners at Buffy's house are quiet moments amid the chaos—Joyce Summers's home-cooked meals offering a brief return to normalcy as Buffy juggles slaying with school. Around the dinner table, secrets surface, tensions rise, and love endures, whether it's with blood relatives or the Slayerettes. This comforting spaghetti with homemade meat sauce is a tribute to those warm meals that remind us what we're fighting for.

Ingredients

2 tablespoons extra-virgin olive oil

1 small yellow onion, finely chopped

1 carrot, peeled and finely chopped

2 garlic cloves, minced, or 1 teaspoon garlic powder

1 teaspoon kosher salt, plus more for seasoning

1 pound lean ground beef

8 ounces hot or sweet Italian sausage

1 tablespoon Italian seasoning

½ teaspoon freshly ground black pepper

3½ cups Marinara Sauce (page 69)

¾ cup water

1 pound spaghetti

Grated Parmesan cheese, for serving

In a heavy Dutch oven or saucepan over medium heat, warm the oil. Add the onion, carrot, garlic, and a pinch of salt and cook, stirring, until lightly browned and softened, about 5 minutes. Add the ground beef and sausage and cook, breaking up the meat with a wooden spoon, until the meat is no longer pink, about 5 minutes. Stir in the Italian seasoning, salt, and pepper, then add the marinara sauce and water and bring to a simmer. Partially cover the pot, reduce the heat to low, and simmer, stirring occasionally, until thickened and flavorful, about 30 minutes.

When the sauce is nearly done, fill a large pot two-thirds full with salted water and bring to a boil over high heat. Add the spaghetti, stir well, and cook, stirring occasionally, until al dente, about 10 minutes or according to the package directions. Scoop out and set aside ¼ cup of the cooking water, then drain the pasta in a colander. Return the pasta to the pot.

Add half of the meat sauce to the pot with the spaghetti and, using tongs, gently toss to coat the noodles evenly, adding some of the reserved pasta water as needed to loosen the sauce.

Divide the spaghetti among individual shallow bowls or plates. Top with more meat sauce. Sprinkle generously with Parmesan and serve at once, passing additional Parmesan at the table.

"YOUR DAD AND I, WE HAVE ALL THE FAITH IN THE WORLD IN YOU. WE'LL ALWAYS BE WITH YOU. YOU'VE GOT A WORLD OF STRENGTH IN YOUR HEART. I KNOW YOU DO."

—MRS. SUMMERS
"NORMAL AGAIN" (SEASON 6, EPISODE 17)

MAKES 6 SERVINGS

Mystery Meat Meat Loaf

Cafeteria food is always a gamble, especially at Sunnydale High School, where all the food in the lunchroom once literally turned into snakes. Amid the screaming and chaos (and Cordelia's unfortunate face bite), even Principal Snyder admits the Hellmouth can't stay hidden forever. This Mystery Meat Meat Loaf is a safer kind of surprise: a bacon- and jalapeño-spiked turkey meat loaf stuffed with gooey melted cheese. Suspicious looking? Maybe. But at least this one won't slither off your plate.

Ingredients

3 thick-cut bacon slices, finely chopped

1 large jalapeño, seeded and finely chopped

½ yellow onion, finely chopped

1½ cups fresh white breadcrumbs

⅓ cup whole milk

¾ cup Marinara Sauce (page 69), divided, plus more warmed sauce for serving

3 large eggs, beaten

1 tablespoon dried oregano

1½ teaspoons kosher salt

½ teaspoon freshly ground black pepper

2 pounds ground dark-meat turkey

1 packed cup (about 5 ounces) shredded low-moisture mozzarella cheese

Position a rack in the upper third of the oven and preheat the oven to 425°F. Line a sheet pan with parchment paper.

In a frying pan over medium heat, cook the bacon, stirring occasionally, until crisp, about 5 minutes. Using a slotted spoon, transfer the bacon to a paper towel. Discard all but 1 tablespoon bacon fat in the pan. Add the jalapeño and onion and cook, stirring, until tender, about 5 minutes. Transfer to a large bowl along with the bacon.

Add the breadcrumbs and milk to the bowl with the bacon mixture and stir to combine. Add ¼ cup of the marinara sauce and the eggs, oregano, salt, and pepper and stir to mix well. Crumble the turkey into the breadcrumb mixture and stir gently until evenly mixed.

Transfer a little more than half of the mixture to the prepared sheet pan and shape it into an oval about 12 inches long and 5 inches wide. Create a hollow in the center, leaving a "wall" about 1 inch thick on the ends and 1 to 2 inches thick on the sides. Pack the shredded mozzarella into the hollow, then use the rest of the meat mixture to top the cheese, working gently and sealing the cheese into the meat loaf.

Bake for 30 minutes. Remove the pan from the oven. Wipe away any oozing protein (this is perfectly natural), then spread the remaining ½ cup marinara sauce over the top and sides of the meat loaf.

Return to the oven and bake until richly browned and an instant-read thermometer inserted in the center registers 165°F, 15 to 20 minutes longer. Let stand for about 10 minutes, then slice and serve warm.

"OH, YEAH, BABY. IT'S SNAKE-A-LICIOUS IN HERE."

—XANDER

"I ONLY HAVE EYES FOR YOU" (SEASON 2, EPISODE 19)

MAKES 4 BURGERS

Doublemeat Palace Burgers

Buffy's stint at the Doublemeat Palace is greasy, grim, and weirdly unforgettable, with her working double shifts, dealing with dead-end coworkers, and suspecting that the "secret ingredient" in the burgers might be human. (Spoiler alert: It's actually a "formed and texturized, vegetable-based meat-like product, suitable for grinding [and] blended with large amounts of rendered beef fat for flavor.") These smash burgers are a safer and tastier alternative: juicy double smash burgers with American cheese, shredded lettuce, grilled onions, and a mystery sauce that won't make you question your humanity. It's fast food, Slayer-style.

Ingredients

Mystery Sauce

½ cup mayonnaise

¼ cup ketchup

1 tablespoon yellow mustard

2 tablespoons finely chopped dill or sweet pickles

½ teaspoon garlic powder

¼ teaspoon freshly ground black pepper

Smash Burgers

2 teaspoons canola oil

1 small red or yellow onion, peeled and sliced paper-thin

Kosher salt

4 tablespoons unsalted butter, at room temperature

4 burger buns

Sliced dill pickles, for topping

Shredded lettuce, for topping

Sliced ripe tomatoes, for topping

1 pound ground beef chuck (preferably 80/20), divided into eight 2-ounce balls

Pinch freshly ground black pepper

4 sandwich-size American or cheddar cheese slices

TO MAKE THE MYSTERY SAUCE: In a small bowl, stir together the mayonnaise, ketchup, mustard, pickles, garlic powder, and pepper. Refrigerate until ready to use.

TO MAKE THE SMASH BURGERS: Heat a heavy griddle or large frying pan (not nonstick) over high heat until very hot. Add the oil and the onion and sprinkle with salt. Sear until nicely browned, stirring occasionally, about 2 minutes. Turn off the heat. Transfer the onions to a plate.

Spread the butter on the cut sides of the burger buns. Return the griddle or pan to medium heat and toast the buns on the cut sides. Arrange the buns on individual plates and spread the cut sides with the mystery sauce. On the bottom bun, layer the pickles and onions. On the top bun, layer lettuce and tomato. (The patties cook quickly, so it's best to have your burger buns ready!)

Heat the griddle or pan over high heat until very hot. Add 2 or more burger balls (without crowding the pan) to the hot griddle or pan. Immediately smash the balls down with a stiff metal spatula, pressing them into thin patties that are just wider than your burger buns. Season generously with salt and pepper. Cook until the patties are well browned, about 45 seconds.

Using the stiff metal spatula, carefully scrape the patties from the griddle or pan, making sure to get all the browned bits, and flip them over. Cook until the other sides of the patties are browned, about 45 seconds longer. Immediately place a slice of cheese on 1 patty and top it with the other patty, then transfer the 2 patties to a bun bottom. Cover with the bun top.

Repeat with the remaining patties and cheese slices and serve immediately.

"BUFFY, YOU KNOW SOMETHING POWERFUL HERE. DO YOU UNDERSTAND THAT? THE DOUBLEMEAT REPUTATION IS BUILT ON A FOUNDATION OF, WELL, MEAT. YOU CAN'T SPREAD THIS AROUND."
—LORRAINE
"DOUBLEMEAT PALACE" (SEASON 6, EPISODE 12)

MAKES 6 SERVINGS

Bewitched Beer-Braised Beef Stew

When Buffy drowns her post-breakup sorrows in cursed campus beer, things get . . . prehistoric. Regressing into "Cave-Slayer" mode, she grunts, breaks furniture, and demands beer. This beer-braised stew is rich and hearty, simmered low and slow in dark beer with herbs and vegetables. It's comfort food with a kick, perfect for when you're feeling a little primal but still want to use utensils.

Ingredients

2½ pounds beef chuck stew meat

1½ teaspoons kosher salt, plus more for seasoning

1 teaspoon freshly ground black pepper, plus more for seasoning

3 tablespoons canola oil

1 yellow onion, chopped

2 large celery stalks, chopped

2 tablespoons unsalted butter

3 garlic cloves, minced

¼ cup all-purpose flour

3 tablespoons tomato paste

One 12-ounce bottle lager-style beer

1 cup chicken broth or beef broth, plus more as needed

2 fresh thyme sprigs

3 carrots, peeled and cut into ¾-inch pieces

1 pound Yukon gold potatoes, cut into ¾-inch pieces

8 ounces small cremini or button mushrooms, halved or quartered

Crusty bread, for serving

Preheat the oven to 325°F.

Pat the meat dry with paper towels, then season all over with ½ teaspoon of the salt and ½ teaspoon of the pepper. In a large Dutch oven over high heat, warm the oil.

Add half of the stew meat to the pot, spreading the pieces into an even layer. Sear until one side is deep brown, about 5 minutes; turn if desired, but as long as you have one nicely browned side it will add lots of flavor. Transfer the meat to a plate. Repeat with the remaining meat.

Reduce the heat to medium and add the onion and celery to the pot. Cook, stirring to scrape up the browned bits on the bottom of the pot, until the vegetables are lightly browned and softened, about 6 minutes. Stir in the butter and garlic until the butter is melted. Stir in the flour until the vegetables are evenly coated.

Stir in the tomato paste until combined, then slowly add the beer, stirring as the mixture thickens and scraping the bottom of the pan to dislodge any browned bits. Add the broth, thyme sprigs, the remaining 1 teaspoon salt, and the remaining ½ teaspoon pepper, and stir well to combine. Bring the mixture to a boil and return the stew meat to the pan. Cover tightly with the lid and place in the oven. Cook for 1 hour.

Add the carrots, potatoes, and mushrooms, stir gently, and re-cover the pan with the lid. Cook until the meat is very tender and the vegetables are tender, about 1 hour longer. Taste and season with additional salt and pepper if needed. Serve with plenty of crusty bread.

"GILES, DON'T MAKE CAVE-SLAYER UNHAPPY."

—XANDER

"BEER BAD" (SEASON 4, EPISODE 5)

MAKES 4 SERVINGS

Roast Turkey Trouble and Yams

Buffy's first Thanksgiving on her own was meant to be traditional: turkey, yams with marshmallows, stuffing, the works. But in true Sunnydale fashion, things go sideways fast when a vengeful Chumash spirit crashes the party. Swords are drawn, arrows fly, and dinner is delayed until midnight. This all-in-one meal is a nod to that chaotic feast: butter-braised turkey breast and honey-glazed yams (with marshmallows, if you dare). Not perfect—but, somehow, just right.

Ingredients

Note: Ask your butcher to tie the turkey breast for roasting.

Brined Turkey Breast

2 quarts water, divided

⅓ cup kosher salt

⅓ packed cup light brown sugar

1 tablespoon whole peppercorns

2 fresh thyme or oregano sprigs

1 boneless turkey breast half, tied (about 2 pounds)

Glaze

¼ cup unsalted butter, melted

1 tablespoon honey

1 teaspoon finely chopped fresh thyme, oregano, or sage

¼ teaspoon kosher salt

TO MAKE THE BRINED TURKEY BREAST: In a large saucepan, combine 1 quart of the water with the salt, brown sugar, peppercorns, and herb sprigs. Bring to a boil, stirring until the salt and sugar are dissolved. Pour the mixture into a bowl just large enough to hold the turkey and the liquid, then add the remaining 1 quart water. Refrigerate until the brine is chilled, about 1 hour.

Add the turkey breast, making sure the breast is submerged (you can weigh it down with a smaller plate). Refrigerate for at least 2 hours or up to overnight, turning occasionally.

TO MAKE THE GLAZE: In a small bowl, stir together the butter, honey, thyme, and salt.

Preheat the oven to 350°F.

TO COOK THE TURKEY: Remove the turkey from the brine and pat it dry with paper towels. Place the turkey, skin side up, on a roasting rack set in a small roasting pan or cast-iron frying pan. Roast, uncovered, for 45 minutes. While the turkey is roasting, baste it 2 or 3 times with the butter mixture.

Turn the oven temperature up to 400°F and continue to roast and baste until golden brown and the internal temperature reads 165°F on an instant-read thermometer inserted into the thickest part of the breast, 30 to 45 minutes longer. Remove from the oven and tent with aluminum foil while you roast the yams.

(Continued on page 86)

YAMS

3 medium sweet potatoes or yams (about 1½ pounds), peeled or unpeeled, cut crosswise into ½-inch-thick slices

2 tablespoons extra-virgin olive oil

½ teaspoon kosher salt

¼ teaspoon freshly ground black pepper

½ cup mini marshmallows (if you must)

TO MAKE THE YAMS: Increase the oven temperature to 450°F. Pile the yams on a baking sheet and drizzle with the olive oil, tossing to coat. Arrange the yams in a single layer on the baking sheet. Season with the salt and pepper. Roast the yams, turning once halfway through cooking, until browned and tender, about 13 minutes. Brush the yams generously with the butter-honey mixture and return to the oven to cook for 5 more minutes. You can top the yams with the marshmallows (if using) at this time so they get melty in the oven.

Just before the yams are ready, carve the turkey and arrange the slices around a large platter, leaving space for the yams. Transfer the yams to the platter (carefully, if you've topped them with marshmallows). Serve at once.

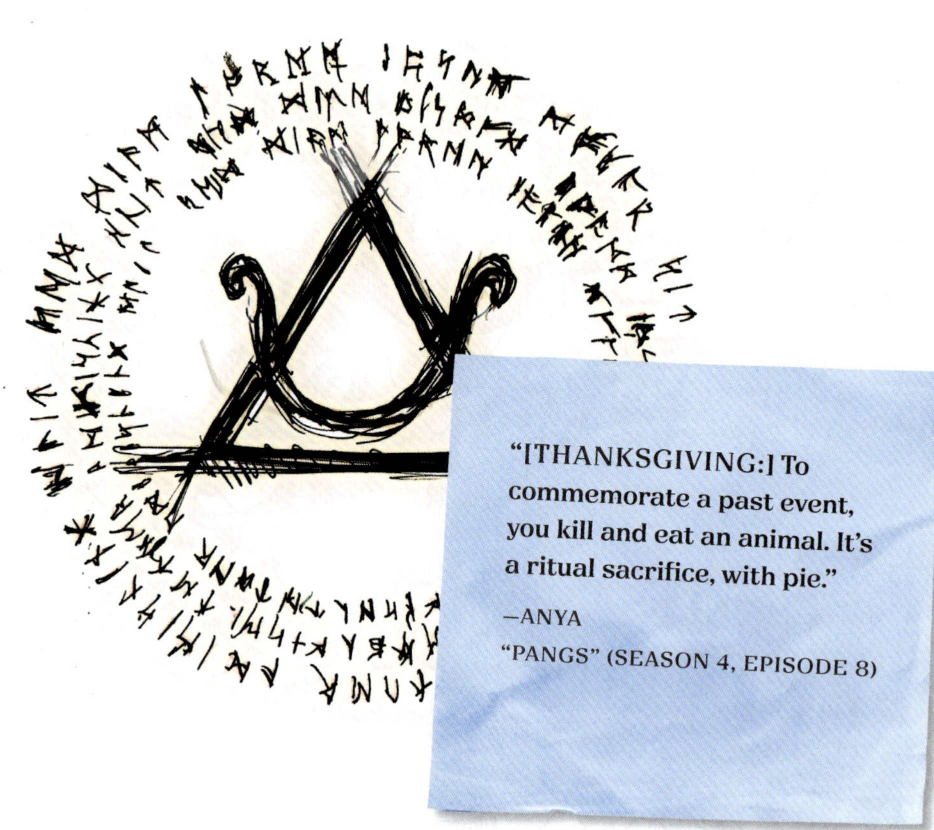

"[THANKSGIVING:] To commemorate a past event, you kill and eat an animal. It's a ritual sacrifice, with pie."

—ANYA

"PANGS" (SEASON 4, EPISODE 8)

MAKES 6 SERVINGS

Homecoming Roast Chicken Dinner

In one of the most haunting episodes of *Buffy the Vampire Slayer*, "Normal Again," Buffy's trapped between two realities—one where she's the Slayer and another where she's a psychiatric patient imagining it all. Her parents plead with her to come back to them, with Mrs. Summers gently reminding Buffy, "You've got people who love you . . . You've got a world of strength in your heart." This Homecoming Roast Chicken Dinner is a nod to that moment—simple, grounding comfort: roasted chicken thighs with peppers, potatoes, and onions, all on one sheet pan, for when reality needs a soft place to land.

Ingredients

1 pound mini sweet peppers or 3 bell peppers (preferably red, orange, and yellow)

1½ pounds small red or yellow potatoes, halved (or quartered if large)

1 red onion, cut into ½-inch-thick wedges

2 tablespoons extra-virgin olive oil, plus more for drizzling

2 tablespoons balsamic vinegar, divided

2 teaspoons kosher salt, divided

1 teaspoon freshly ground black pepper, divided

6 large bone-in, skin-on chicken thighs (about 3 pounds)

1 tablespoon Italian seasoning, divided

¼ cup roughly chopped fresh basil

Position a rack in the upper third of the oven and preheat the oven to 400°F. Halve the peppers, then use a spoon to scoop out the seeds and membranes. If using larger bell peppers, cut them into chunks.

On a large-rimmed baking sheet, combine the peppers, potatoes, and onion. Drizzle with the oil and 1 tablespoon of the vinegar, season with 1 teaspoon of the salt and ½ teaspoon of the pepper, and toss to coat evenly. Spread into an even layer on the baking sheet.

Season the bottoms of the chicken thighs with 1½ teaspoons of the Italian seasoning, ½ teaspoon of the salt, and ¼ teaspoon of the pepper. Arrange the chicken pieces on top of the vegetables, skin sides up. Season the skin sides of the chicken thighs with the remaining Italian seasoning, salt, and pepper, then drizzle them with olive oil.

Roast until the chicken is nicely browned and cooked through and the veggies are tender and caramelized, moving the chicken around (keep it skin side up) and stirring the veggies a few times, about 45 minutes.

Transfer to a serving platter. Sprinkle with the basil and drizzle the remaining 1 tablespoon vinegar over everything before serving.

"YOU'RE OUR LITTLE GIRL, BUFFY, OUR ONE AND ONLY."

—MRS. SUMMERS, "NORMAL AGAIN" (SEASON 6, EPISODE 17)

MAKES 4 SERVINGS

Doppelgänger Fish Tacos

Salty and sweet, tangy and creamy, these grilled and blackened fish tacos with mango-pineapple-lime salsa and avocado crema play on the idea of duality, mirroring the contrasting versions of Willow—her usual sweet, nerdy self and her seductive, villainous vampire counterpart. In the episode "Doppelgängland" in Season 3, Buffy and the real Willow must save the day when, from the bleak alternate universe where vampires rule Sunnydale, Willow's bloodsucking doppelgänger is brought forth and wreaks havoc and confusion on the town. Evil Willow eventually gets the stake but not without the help of all the Slayerettes.

Ingredients

Fish Tacos

1 pound cod or snapper fillets, skin and pinbones removed

1 tablespoon blackened seasoning

2 tablespoons canola oil

8 corn tortillas, warmed

Lime wedges, for serving

Avocado Crema

½ avocado, pitted, peeled, and cut into chunks

½ cup Mexican crema or sour cream

Finely grated zest and juice of 1 lime

2 tablespoons chopped fresh cilantro

Kosher salt

Freshly ground black pepper

Place the fish fillets on a baking sheet and season liberally on both sides with the blackened seasoning. Refrigerate uncovered for at least 30 minutes or up to 2 hours.

TO MAKE THE AVOCADO CREMA: Combine the avocado, crema, lime zest and juice, and cilantro in a blender and blend on medium speed until very smooth. Transfer to a small bowl and season to taste with salt and pepper. Refrigerate until ready to use.

(Continued on page 91)

CHEERLEADER TRYOUTS

SHS

PARENT-TEACHER NIGHT

GO SUNNYDALE!

CAREER DAY

FIELD TRIP TO THE ZOO

DON'T FORGET YOUR PERMISSION SLIPS!

Mango-Pineapple Salsa

½ cup diced ripe mango

½ cup diced fresh pineapple

½ red Fresno chile, seeded and minced

1½ tablespoons chopped fresh cilantro

1 tablespoon minced red onion

Juice of 1 lime

2 teaspoons canola oil

Kosher salt

Special Equipment

Blender

TO MAKE THE MANGO-PINEAPPLE SALSA: In a medium bowl, combine the mango, pineapple, chile, cilantro, onion, lime juice, and oil, then season to taste with salt. Refrigerate until ready to use.

TO MAKE THE FISH TACOS: In a large, heavy frying pan over medium-high heat, warm the canola oil. Add the fish fillets in a single layer, in batches if necessary to avoid overcrowding. Cook until the bottom side of the fish is nicely browned, then turn and sear the other side, until the fish is cooked through and flaky, 3 to 5 minutes depending on the thickness of the fish.

Divide the tortillas among four individual plates. Gently flake the fish into large chunks and divide it evenly among the tortillas. Dollop the avocado crema over the fish, then spoon the salsa on top. Serve at once, with lime wedges on the side.

"THAT'S ME AS A VAMPIRE? I'M SO EVIL AND SKANKY."

—WILLOW
"DOPPELGÄNGLAND" (SEASON 3, EPISODE 16)

MAKES 4 SERVINGS

Tied-Up Salmon

Spike spends most of Thanksgiving tied to a chair, whining about not being fed while arrows fly and chaos reigns. "I'm too hungry to remember everything." This dish is a cheeky nod to his predicament: salmon fillets wrapped and tied in parchment with herb butter, spiral-cut zucchini, and fresh cherry tomatoes. It's elegant, flavorful, and—unlike Spike's meal—actually served.

Ingredients

4 tablespoons unsalted butter, at room temperature

1 tablespoon mixed chopped fresh herbs, such as dill, chives, and basil

Kosher salt and freshly ground black pepper

2 cups spiral-cut zucchini

4 thin salmon fillets (each about 6 ounces), skin and pinbones removed

1 cup quartered cherry tomatoes

1 lemon, cut into 6 wedges

Special Equipment

Kitchen twine

Preheat the oven to 400°F. Cut out four pieces of parchment paper, each about 12 inches square. In a medium bowl, stir together the butter, herbs, and a pinch each of salt and pepper.

Divide the zucchini evenly among the parchment pieces, placing it in the center of each piece. Season with a little salt. Top each with a salmon fillet. Season each fillet lightly with salt and pepper, then spread each with some of the butter mixture, dividing it evenly among the fillets.

Scatter the cherry tomatoes over the fillets, dividing them evenly, then squeeze the juice from 2 wedges of the lemon over the top.

Lift two sides of the parchment paper to meet in the middle above the fish fillet. Tightly roll the paper down to meet the fish, then crimp and roll the ends, tucking them underneath the package to seal. Tie the packets with kitchen twine.

Place the packets on a baking sheet in a single layer. Bake until the fish is just cooked through but still juicy, about 20 minutes.

Transfer each packet to a plate, untie, and serve.

"BLOODY HELL, WOMAN. YOU'RE CUTTIN' OFF MY CIRCULATION."

—SPIKE

"PANGS" (SEASON 4, EPISODE 8)

MAKES 4 SERVINGS

The Chosen Curry

Buffy is the Chosen One, tasked with standing alone against the darkness, making impossible choices, and carrying a weight few can understand. This comforting vegetarian curry is a tribute to her strength and balance. Chickpeas, sweet potatoes, and spinach simmer in warming spices and coconut milk. The Chosen Curry is nourishing, bold, and quietly powerful, much like the Slayer herself.

Ingredients

1 tablespoon extra-virgin olive oil

1 small yellow onion, finely chopped

½ teaspoon kosher salt, plus a pinch, divided, plus more for seasoning

2 garlic cloves, minced

2 teaspoons grated peeled fresh ginger

1 teaspoon ground cumin

1 teaspoon ground coriander

1 teaspoon ground turmeric

½ teaspoon red pepper flakes (or more, if desired)

Pinch ground cardamom

¼ teaspoon freshly ground black pepper, plus more for seasoning

1 cup water

1 sweet potato (about 8 ounces), peeled and cubed

One 15-ounce can chickpeas, drained and rinsed

One 13.5-ounce can coconut milk

Juice of 1 small lemon, plus more as needed

2 packed cups (about 3 ounces) chopped fresh baby spinach

¼ cup chopped fresh cilantro

Steamed rice or warm naan, for serving

Plain yogurt, for serving

In a large, heavy saucepan or Dutch oven over medium heat, warm the oil. Add the onion and a pinch of salt and cook, stirring, until soft and lightly browned, about 5 minutes. Add the remaining ½ teaspoon salt and the garlic, ginger, cumin, coriander, turmeric, red pepper flakes, cardamom, and pepper and stir to combine. Pour in the water and bring to a boil.

Add the sweet potato, chickpeas, coconut milk, and lemon juice to the pot. Return the mixture to a boil, then reduce the heat to low and simmer, partially covered and stirring occasionally, until the sweet potato pieces are tender but not mushy, about 25 minutes.

Taste and adjust the seasoning with more salt, pepper, or lemon. Add the spinach and cilantro. Cook until the curry is warmed through and the spinach is wilted. Serve hot with rice or naan and yogurt.

MAKES 4 TO 6 SERVINGS

Demon's Delight Pasta

Anya may be awkward and overly enthusiastic about capitalism, but beneath the surface lies someone genuinely struggling to understand what it means to be human. As an ex-vengeance demon who hasn't been mortal in over a thousand years, she wrestles with the fragility of life, the messiness of emotions, and the strange customs of modern society. Demon's Delight Pasta captures her fiery spirit with a bold arrabbiata sauce, Calabrian chiles, and plenty of garlic. It is intense and unapologetically unforgettable, just like Anya.

Ingredients

One 12-ounce jar roasted red peppers, drained

2 tablespoons extra-virgin olive oil

½ yellow onion, finely chopped

1 teaspoon kosher salt, plus a pinch, divided

4 to 6 garlic cloves, minced

2 tablespoons finely chopped Calabrian peppers or 2 teaspoons red pepper flakes

One 28-ounce can crushed San Marzano tomatoes

⅓ cup water

½ teaspoon freshly ground black pepper

1 pound rigatoni or penne pasta

Grated Parmesan cheese, for garnish

Chopped fresh basil, for garnish

Special Equipment

Blender

In a blender, purée the roasted red peppers. Set aside.

In a large, heavy saucepan or Dutch oven over medium heat, warm the oil. Add the onion and a big pinch of salt and cook, stirring, until lightly golden and softened, about 6 minutes. Add the garlic and Calabrian peppers and cook until fragrant, about 1 minute. Add the remaining 1 teaspoon salt and the puréed roasted red peppers, crushed tomatoes, water, and pepper.

Bring the sauce to a simmer, then reduce the heat to low and let simmer gently, uncovered and stirring occasionally, until the sauce thickens, about 30 minutes. Cover to keep warm.

Fill a large pot two-thirds full with salted water and bring to a boil over high heat. Add the rigatoni, stir well, and cook, stirring occasionally, until al dente, about 10 minutes or according to the package directions. Scoop out and set aside ½ cup of the cooking water. Drain the pasta in a colander, then add it back to the pot.

Add a few cups of the sauce to the hot pasta and gently toss to coat evenly, adding some of the reserved pasta water if needed to loosen the sauce.

Divide the pasta among warm individual bowls or plates. Top with more sauce and garnish with Parmesan and basil. Serve.

"FOR A THOUSAND YEARS I WIELDED THE POWERS OF THE WISH. I BROUGHT RUIN TO THE HEADS OF UNFAITHFUL MEN. I BROUGHT FORTH DESTRUCTION AND CHAOS FOR THE PLEASURE OF THE LOWER BEINGS. I WAS FEARED AND WORSHIPPED ACROSS THE GLOBE, AND NOW I'M STUCK AT SUNNYDALE HIGH."

—ANYA

"DOPPELGÄNGLAND" (SEASON 3, EPISODE 16)

MAKES 12 PASTRIES

Twisted Prophecy Pastries

Ground beef (or turkey) picadillo filling blends sweet and savory with green olives, bell peppers, spices, and currants. The rich, complex flavor of these pastries mirrors the shifting nature of Buffy's prophecies, which rarely unfold as expected. When Giles discovers an ancient prophecy foretelling Buffy's death at the hands of the Master, she struggles with her fate and even tries to quit as Slayer. In the end, she accepts the inevitable and faces the Master, only to defeat him even after dying, telling him, "I may be dead, but I'm still pretty. Which is more than I can say for you."

Ingredients

Dough

3 cups all-purpose flour, plus more for dusting

¾ teaspoon kosher salt

10 tablespoons cold unsalted butter, diced

2 large egg yolks

9 tablespoons ice cold water, plus more as needed

1 tablespoon distilled white vinegar

Picadillo

1 tablespoon extra-virgin olive oil

1 small yellow onion, finely chopped

½ green bell pepper, seeded and diced

½ red bell pepper, seeded and diced

½ teaspoon kosher salt, plus a pinch, divided, plus more as needed

1 pound ground beef

¼ cup tomato paste

2 tablespoons hot pepper sauce

TO MAKE THE DOUGH: Combine the flour and salt in a food processor and pulse a few times to mix. Add the butter and process just until the butter pieces are the size of peas. In a small bowl, mix together the egg yolks, water, and vinegar. Add to the flour mixture and pulse just until moistened. The dough should hold together when pressed; if it doesn't, add a little more water. Dump the dough onto a clean work surface and press it together, then divide it into 2 large disks. Refrigerate for at least 30 minutes or up to 1 day.

TO MAKE THE PICADILLO: In a large frying pan over medium heat, warm the oil. Add the onion and green and red peppers and a pinch of salt and cook, stirring, until the onion is tender and golden, about 6 minutes. Crumble the meat into the pan, then increase the heat to medium-high. Cook, stirring occasionally to break up the meat, until the meat is no longer pink, about 3 minutes. Pour off most of the fat from the pan.

Return the pan to medium heat and add the tomato paste, hot pepper sauce, cumin, oregano, the remaining ½ teaspoon salt, and the pepper and cook, stirring, until the flavors come together, about 2 minutes. Remove from the heat. Add the currants, olives, and honey to the meat mixture and stir to combine. Taste and season with more salt and pepper if needed. Let cool to room temperature or transfer to an airtight container and refrigerate until ready to use, up to 3 days.

(Continued on page 99)

1 teaspoon ground cumin

1 teaspoon dried Mexican oregano

¼ teaspoon freshly ground black pepper, plus more as needed

½ cup dried currants or raisins

½ cup sliced pimiento-stuffed green olives

1 teaspoon honey

1 large egg beaten with 1 teaspoon water, for egg wash

Line 2 rimmed baking sheets with parchment paper. On a lightly floured work surface, roll out the dough into a round 1/8 inch thick. Using a large round cutter that is approximately 5½ inches in diameter (or a stencil and a paring knife), cut out as many rounds as you can. Gather the dough scraps, roll them out, and cut out additional shapes (if the dough becomes too warm, refrigerate it for about 15 minutes). You should have 12 rounds. Transfer the rounds to a baking sheet and refrigerate for 15 minutes.

Lay the dough rounds on a clean work surface. Brush one half of each round lightly with the egg wash. Place about ¼ cup of the filling in the center of each shape, leaving a ½-inch border. Fold a round over into a half circle. Press around the edges to enclose the filling, then use the tines of a fork to seal the pastries. Transfer the pastries to the prepared baking sheets, spacing them at least 1 inch apart. Refrigerate for 15 minutes. (The pastries can be refrigerated at this point for up to 1 day.)

While the pastries chill, position 2 racks evenly in the middle of the oven and preheat the oven to 375°F.

Brush the pastries with the egg wash. Bake until golden brown, 25 to 30 minutes. Remove from the oven and let cool for 5 minutes on the baking sheets on wire racks. Transfer the pastries to a platter and serve warm.

"TOMORROW NIGHT, BUFFY WILL FACE THE MASTER, AND SHE WILL DIE."

—GILES
"PROPHECY GIRL"
(SEASON 1, EPISODE 12)

MAKES 4 TO 6 SERVINGS

Slay Day Garlic Veggie Noodles

Sitting at the kitchen island, eating Chinese takeout while arguing about driving tests in between apocalypse-level threats is about as *Buffy* as it gets. Buffy and Joyce Summers's banter over noodles is funny, tense, and achingly normal—a reminder that, for all the world-saving, sometimes the real fight is just convincing your mom to hand over the keys. This easy noodle dish channels that everyday warmth with garlic-soy comfort and plenty of veggies. Add cubes of tofu or sliced chicken or beef to the mix if you need more protein to slay.

Ingredients

Sauce

4 garlic cloves, minced

2 green onions, white and green parts, thinly sliced

2 teaspoons grated peeled fresh ginger or 1 teaspoon ground ginger

3 tablespoons reduced-sodium tamari or soy sauce

2 tablespoons rice vinegar

1 packed tablespoon light brown sugar

2 teaspoons sriracha (or more, if desired)

1 teaspoon toasted sesame oil

1 teaspoon cornstarch

Stir-Fry

1 tablespoon kosher salt

1 pound fresh Chinese or Korean noodles

2 tablespoons canola oil

2 cups (about 6 ounces) small broccoli florets

1 large carrot, peeled and cut into matchsticks

1 small red bell pepper, stemmed, seeded, and cut into small slices

8 ounces cremini, button, and/or shiitake mushrooms, thickly sliced

½ cup chopped toasted salted cashews (optional)

TO MAKE THE SAUCE: In a small bowl, whisk together the garlic, green onions, ginger, tamari, rice vinegar, brown sugar, sriracha, sesame oil, and cornstarch. Set aside.

TO MAKE THE STIR-FRY: Bring a large pot of water to a boil and add the salt. Add the noodles to the boiling water and cook until al dente, according to the package directions. Drain.

Meanwhile, in a wok or large frying pan over medium-high heat, warm the oil until it shimmers. Add the broccoli, carrot, bell pepper, and mushrooms and cook, stirring and tossing, until crisp-tender, about 7 minutes.

Add the sauce and toss to coat the vegetables, then add the noodles to the pan. Stir-fry, tossing the mixture together, until warmed through and well combined, about 2 minutes.

Divide the stir-fry among bowls, sprinkle each serving with the cashews (if using), and serve.

"I SPEND ENOUGH TIME NOT KNOWING WHERE YOU ARE. I DON'T WANT TO ADD TO THAT THE POSSIBILITY THAT YOU'RE ON THE HIGHWAY TO CHICAGO."

—MRS. SUMMERS
"BAND CANDY" (SEASON 3, EPISODE 6)

CHAPTER FIVE

SWEET FANGS

"HOW COME YOU DIDN'T TELL ME I LOOK LIKE A CRAZY BIRTHDAY CAKE IN THIS SHIRT?"

—WILLOW

"WILD AT HEART" (SEASON 4, EPISODE 6)

When Willow's in the kitchen, you know the magic isn't just in the spellbook. It's in every sprinkle, swirl, and sugar-dusted bite. These Slayerettes-approved sweets, from cookies and cake to pie and other confections, are perfect for post-ritual sugar rushes, recharging after a night of vamp dusting, or distracting a demon long enough to pull the old "run away really fast" maneuver. Just remember, in Sunnydale, even dessert can be a little . . . bite-y.

MILKBAR
MILK CHOCOLATE

MAKES ABOUT 12 OUNCES BARK

Cursed Chocolate Bark

This sweet-and-sinister treat plays on the chaos of cursed chocolate turning Sunnydale's adults into wild, unsupervised teens. One minute Mrs. Summers and Giles are responsible authority figures and the next they're sneaking around and lighting up like it's senior year. Snappy, nut- and cherry-studded chocolate bark recalls the infamous candy at the heart of the mayhem: deceptively simple, dangerously irresistible, and best consumed without any magical side effects.

Ingredients

- 8 ounces bittersweet or semisweet chocolate chips
- ½ cup chopped toasted almonds or pistachios (or a mixture), divided
- ½ cup pitted dried sour cherries, divided

Line a rimmed 13-by-18-inch baking sheet with parchment paper.

Put the chocolate chips in a microwavable bowl. Melt the chocolate in the microwave in 30-second bursts, stirring after each 30 seconds, until melted and smooth.

Stir half of the almonds and half of the cherries into the melted chocolate, then scrape the mixture onto the prepared baking sheet. Use a small metal spatula to spread it into an even layer; the rectangle or oval should be about 7 by 10 inches.

Immediately sprinkle the chocolate with the remaining nuts and cherries, then gently press down on the nuts and fruit to adhere them to the chocolate.

Refrigerate the bark, uncovered, until firm, about 1 hour.

Gently peel the bark from the parchment paper, then break it into large, irregular pieces. Serve.

"GILES AT SIXTEEN. LESS 'TOGETHER GUY,' MORE 'BAD MAGIC, HATES THE WORLD, TICKING TIME BOMB GUY.'"

—BUFFY
"BAND CANDY"
(SEASON 3, EPISODE 6)

MAKES 8 SERVINGS

Angel's Food Cake

Light as air but not without weight, this cake mirrors the bittersweet reveal at the heart of Buffy and Angel's early romance. When Buffy first learns the truth about Angel's vampire identity, what begins as a tender moment between them quickly spirals into something darker. Angel confesses his hunger to her, highlighting the danger lurking just below his calm demeanor. Serve this cake in thick slices, with blood-red berries or blood orange segments and plenty of whipped cream, for a dessert that's as sweet and intense as Buffy and Angel's relationship.

Ingredients

9 large egg whites, at room temperature

1 teaspoon cream of tartar

¼ teaspoon kosher salt

1½ cups sugar, divided

2 teaspoons pure vanilla extract

¼ teaspoon almond extract

1 cup (about 4½ ounces) cake flour

Special Equipment

Stand mixer

10-inch footed tube pan with removable bottom

Position an oven rack in the lower third of the oven and preheat the oven to 350°F.

In the bowl of a stand mixer fitted with the whisk attachment, combine the egg whites, cream of tartar, and salt. Beat on medium-high speed until the mixture is foamy, then slowly add 1 cup of the sugar while beating. Add the vanilla and almond extracts and continue to beat until stiff peaks form (do not overbeat or the cake will be dry).

Sift the flour and the remaining ½ cup sugar over the whipped egg whites and gently fold the dry ingredients into the egg whites.

Gently spoon the mixture into an ungreased 10-inch footed tube pan with a removable bottom. Bake until the top is golden brown and the cake is cooked through, about 35 minutes.

Remove the cake from the oven and immediately invert the pan onto the countertop (the cake needs to cool upside down or it will collapse). Let the cake cool completely, about 1 hour.

Run a long, thin knife around the sides and center of the tube pan. Remove the cake from the pan, inverting it onto a serving plate. Serve in thick slices.

"I CAN WALK LIKE A MAN, BUT I'M NOT ONE. I WANTED TO KILL YOU TONIGHT."

—ANGEL
"ANGEL" (SEASON 1, EPISODE 7)

MAKES 16 COOKIES

Magical Chaos Cookies

These kitchen-sink cookies are irresistible, packed with chocolate chips, candy-coated chocolate pieces, marshmallows, sprinkles, and crushed chocolate sandwich cookies. After Oz leaves to figure out his werewolf nature, a heartbroken Willow casts a spell to make her will be done and distracts herself by baking. But when the spell backfires, everything she says starts coming true. Cue the inevitable magical mayhem, accidental engagements, and demon trouble. To make things right, Willow bakes batch after batch of cookies in apology, hoping a million chips might undo the damage (it doesn't).

Ingredients

½ cup unsalted butter, at room temperature

1 packed cup light brown sugar

⅓ cup granulated sugar

½ teaspoon kosher salt

1 large egg, plus 1 large egg yolk

2 teaspoons pure vanilla extract

2 cups unbleached all-purpose flour

1 teaspoon baking soda

½ teaspoon baking powder

¾ cup chocolate chips

¾ cup mini marshmallows

½ cup candy-coated chocolate pieces

12 chocolate sandwich cookies, roughly crushed

¼ cup rainbow sprinkles

Special Equipment

Stand mixer

Position 2 oven racks evenly in the oven and preheat the oven to 375°F. Line 2 large-rimmed baking sheets with parchment paper.

In the bowl of a stand mixer fitted with the paddle attachment, beat the butter, brown sugar, granulated sugar, and salt on medium speed until creamy and well combined. Add the whole egg, egg yolk, and vanilla and beat until well combined. Scrape down the sides of the bowl. Add the flour, baking soda, and baking powder and beat on low speed just until blended. Add the chocolate chips, marshmallows, candy-coated chocolate pieces, chocolate sandwich cookies, and sprinkles and mix on low speed just until combined.

Scoop up about 2 tablespoons of dough, roll it into a loose ball, and place it on one of the prepared baking sheets. Repeat with the remaining dough, placing 8 dough balls on each baking sheet, spacing them apart. Press each ball lightly into a disk about 1 inch thick.

Bake until the cookies are light golden brown and cooked but still soft in the middle, rotating the pans halfway through, about 12 minutes.

Let the cookies cool on the pans for 5 minutes, then transfer them to a wire rack to cool completely. Store in an airtight container at room temperature for up to 5 days.

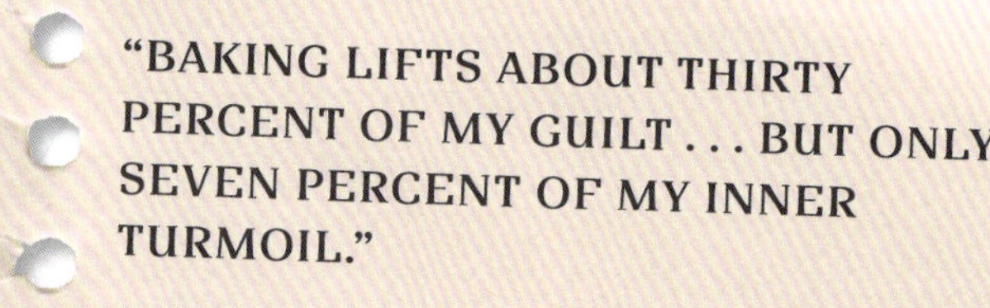

MAKES ONE 9-INCH PIE

Diner Peach Pie

During her self-imposed exile in Los Angeles, Buffy works as a waitress at a rundown diner, trying to escape her past. But when she meets a group of teens struggling to survive and debating whether to spend their limited change on cake or pie, she is reminded of her family, friends, and true calling. This peach pie, with its tender fruit, flaky crust, and hint of cinnamon, is likely better than what Helen's Kitchen served. Use an all-butter crust for the best results, and don't forget the ice cream.

Ingredients

All-purpose flour, for dusting

2 rounds pie dough for a 9-inch pie, thawed if frozen

¾ cup sugar

3 tablespoons tapioca starch

¼ teaspoon ground cinnamon

Pinch kosher salt

6 or 7 ripe but firm peaches, peeled, pitted, and cut into ½-inch-thick slices

1 tablespoon cold unsalted butter, cut into pieces

On a lightly floured surface, roll each dough round into a circle about 12 inches in diameter and about ⅛ inch thick. Line a 9-inch pie pan with one of the rounds. Place the second dough round on a baking sheet lined with parchment paper, and refrigerate both rounds while you prepare the filling.

In a large bowl, whisk together the sugar, tapioca starch, cinnamon, and salt. Add the peach slices and toss to combine. Transfer the peach mixture to the dough-lined pie pan. Dot the peaches with the butter.

Position the second dough round over the filled pie. Trim the edges, leaving a slight overhang, then fold them together and crimp to seal. Cut 5 or 6 slits in the top. Refrigerate the assembled pie while you preheat the oven.

Preheat the oven to 375°F. Bake the pie until the filling is thick and bubbling and the crust is golden brown, about 1 hour. Transfer the pie to a wire rack and let it cool completely before serving.

"WE'VE GOT A PEACH PIE. I CAN'T GUARANTEE THERE'S A PEACH IN IT."

—BUFFY

"ANNE" (SEASON 3, EPISODE 1)

MAKES 12 BARS

Mind-Reading Strawberry Dream Bars

These strawberry dream bars, made with strawberry gelatin, whipped cream cheese, and a graham cracker crust, are cool, creamy, and just the dessert you might find in a high school cafeteria. In the episode "Earshot," as Buffy struggles to stay sane while hearing everyone's thoughts, Xander picks at some gelatin dessert in the cafeteria and accidentally discovers that the lunch lady is lacing food with rat poison. She calls the students vermin and comes after him with a cleaver—until Buffy steps in, just in time, to the save the day. Phew!

Ingredients

Crust

4 tablespoons unsalted butter, melted, plus more for the pan

1 cup finely crushed graham crackers (from about 12 crackers)

3 tablespoons granulated sugar

Pinch kosher salt

Filling

3 ounces strawberry gelatin

¾ cup boiling water

¾ cup cold water

TO MAKE THE CRUST: Preheat the oven to 350°F. Lightly butter an 8-inch-square pan.

In a medium bowl, stir together the graham cracker crumbs, granulated sugar, melted butter, and salt until well combined. Press the mixture evenly into the bottom of the prepared pan, using a flat-bottomed glass to press the mixture firmly together.

Bake the crust until set and golden brown, about 12 minutes. Transfer the pan to a wire rack and let cool completely, then refrigerate until chilled (the crust can be made up to 1 day in advance).

TO MAKE THE FILLING: In a mixing bowl, whisk together the strawberry gelatin and boiling water until the gelatin is dissolved. Add the cold water and stir to combine. Refrigerate until completely cooled but not set, about 10 minutes.

(Continued on page 114)

MAGIC

"VERMIN! YOU'RE ALL VERMIN. YOU COME IN HERE AND YOU EAT, AND YOU EAT. FILTH!"

—LUNCH LADY
"EARSHOT" (SEASON 3, EPISODE 18)

12 ounces cream cheese, at room temperature, divided

1/3 cup powdered sugar

1 teaspoon pure vanilla extract

1 cup heavy whipping cream

Whipped cream, for serving (optional)

Sliced strawberries, for serving (optional)

In a clean mixing bowl, beat 8 ounces of the cream cheese until smooth. With a hand-held electric mixer on low speed, slowly add the chilled gelatin mixture. Beat until smooth and silky. Cover the bowl and refrigerate until the mixture is chilled and thickened but not set, about 30 minutes.

Just before the gelatin mixture is ready, in a clean mixing bowl, beat the remaining 4 ounces of cream cheese with the powdered sugar and vanilla until soft and creamy. Add the heavy cream and beat to medium-stiff peaks.

Add the gelatin mixture and beat on low speed until completely combined and smooth. Pour the filling over the cold crust in an even layer. Refrigerate until set, at least 8 hours or preferably overnight.

To serve, run a large knife under hot water, dry it off, and then slice through the bars to make clean cuts; repeat heating the knife and drying it for every cut. Use a thin metal spatula to remove the bars from the pan. Serve with whipped cream and sliced strawberries (if using).

MAKES 9 SQUARES

Marshmallow Cereal Treats

A sweet, sticky mess of cornflakes, toasted oats cereal, and crisped rice cereal bound by melted marshmallows and salted caramel—just the treat you'd expect to find in the bustling Summers' kitchen. In the episode "Storyteller," Andrew makes a documentary about the apocalypse, offering viewers his romanticized version of life before the end: Buffy pouring cereal like a femme fatale, Spike strutting by shirtless, Anya snacking on grapes like a goddess. But behind the fantasy, it's cereal for dinner and stress for dessert as Buffy strategizes against an oncoming army of evil while Andrew hides in the bathroom.

Ingredients

½ tablespoon granulated sugar

½ cup unsalted butter

¾ packed cup dark brown sugar

⅓ cup heavy cream

2 teaspoons flaky sea salt, divided

One 1-pound bag mini marshmallows (about 8 cups)

3 cups crisped rice cereal

2 cups cornflakes cereal

2 cups toasted oats cereal

Line a 9-inch-square pan with a piece of parchment paper so that 2 edges slightly overhang. Sprinkle the granulated sugar over the bottom of the pan.

In a large pot over medium heat, melt the butter. Add the brown sugar, cream, and 1½ teaspoons of the flaky sea salt. Bring to a simmer, stirring until the sugar dissolves and the mixture thickens, about 1 minute.

Reduce the heat to low. Add the marshmallows and stir until they are completely melted. Remove the saucepan from the heat.

Add the cereals to the pot and stir gently but quickly to combine. Transfer the mixture to the prepared pan and carefully press the mixture into an even layer (using a buttered piece of parchment paper works well). Sprinkle the remaining ½ teaspoon flaky sea salt over the top.

Let the mixture sit at room temperature until firm, about 1 hour, or refrigerate for 30 minutes. Cut into squares and serve.

"THINGS ARE TENSE IN COMMAND CENTRAL THIS MORNING. BUFFY IS CLEARLY CONCERNED WITH SOME UNKNOWN DANGER, AND THE AIR IS FILLED WITH FOREBODING."

—ANDREW

"STORYTELLER" (SEASON 7, EPISODE 16)

"YOU MAY BE
HOT STUFF WHEN
IT COMES TO
DEMONOLOGY . . .
BUT WHEN IT COMES
TO DATING, *I'M* THE
SLAYER."
—CORDELIA
"HALLOWEEN"
(SEASON 2, EPISODE 6)

MAKES 16 TO 18 TRUFFLES

Chocolate Obsession Truffles

Unapologetically indulgent, these chocolate truffles reflect Cordelia's flair for luxury and her obsession with appearances. In the episode "Out of Mind, Out of Sight," she offers chocolates to the popular crowd in exchange for their May Queen, but snubs Buffy, labeling her part of the "loony fringe." Petty? Yes. But undeniably iconic. These treats are for anyone who enjoys a little drama with their dessert.

Ingredients

¼ cup heavy cream

4 tablespoons unsalted butter, diced

8 ounces bittersweet chocolate, chopped

½ teaspoon pure vanilla extract

3 tablespoons Dutch-process cocoa powder, sifted

In a saucepan over medium-low heat, warm the cream just until steaming; do not let it boil. Add the butter and chocolate to the saucepan and stir gently until the mixture is very smooth.

Remove the pan from the heat, stir in the vanilla, and then transfer the mixture to a bowl. Let it cool for 15 minutes. Cover the bowl and refrigerate until the chocolate mixture solidifies, at least 4 hours or overnight.

Using a large melon baller or a tablespoon measure, scoop up about 1 big tablespoon of the chocolate mixture to make rough balls. Place each scoop of truffle mixture onto a large plate. (It's OK if they look rough; this is messy business!)

Put the cocoa powder in a shallow bowl. Working with 1 truffle at a time, press and roll the truffle into a ball (they don't need to be perfect), then roll the ball in the cocoa until completely coated. Transfer to a serving plate.

The truffles can be covered and refrigerated for up to 1 week.

MAKES 4 SERVINGS

Cookie Dough of the Damned

In the series finale, "Chosen," Buffy has a sweet moment with Angel, telling him that she's just like cookie dough—not yet finished, still figuring herself out. This edible cookie dough is a nod to Buffy's "I'm cookie dough" metaphor and that moment of vulnerability and honesty. Facing love, apocalypse, and two soulful vampires, she admits she's not ready to choose a future. But she hasn't given up hope: "I make it through this, and the next thing, and the next thing, and maybe one day, I turn around and realize I'm ready. I'm cookies."

Ingredients

Note: You can heat-treat the flour before using it by spreading it evenly on a microwave-safe plate and microwaving on high for 1 minute.

4 tablespoons unsalted butter, at room temperature

½ packed cup light brown sugar

2 tablespoons granulated sugar

Pinch ground cinnamon

¼ teaspoon kosher salt

2 tablespoons whole milk

1 teaspoon pure vanilla extract

1 cup all-purpose flour

½ cup chocolate chips

Special Equipment

Stand mixer

In the bowl of a stand mixer fitted with the paddle attachment, beat the butter, brown sugar, granulated sugar, cinnamon, and salt on medium speed until creamy and well combined. Add the milk and vanilla and beat until well combined. Scrape down the sides of the bowl. Add the heat-treated flour and beat on low speed just until blended. Add the chocolate chips.

Cover and refrigerate for at least 30 minutes, then serve. Store in an airtight container in the refrigerator for up to 5 days.

"I'M COOKIE DOUGH. I'M NOT DONE BAKING. I'M NOT FINISHED BECOMING . . . WHOEVER THE HELL IT IS I'M GONNA TURN OUT TO BE."

– BUFFY
"CHOSEN" (SEASON 7, EPISODE 22)

PLURIBUS UNUM
1881

MAKES ABOUT 12 LARGE BROWNIES

Witch Hunt Brownies

Amy's mother, Catherine "the Great," is a harsh, controlling former cheer queen whose strict "broth kicks" drive Amy to seek comfort with Willow and their secret brownie stash. Just like Buffy unravelling the deadly witch's curse affecting Sunnydale's cheerleading squad, these peanut butter–swirled dark chocolate brownies offer a sweet but fiery reminder of resilience and friendship. Use natural peanut butter with only peanuts and salt for the best result (it's runnier than the no-stir version, which contains added oils).

Ingredients

Nonstick cooking spray

4 large eggs

1¼ cups unsweetened natural cocoa powder

1 teaspoon baking powder

1 teaspoon kosher salt

½ teaspoon cayenne pepper (optional)

1 cup unsalted butter

2 cups sugar

1 tablespoon pure vanilla extract

1½ cups all-purpose flour

1½ cups semisweet chocolate chips

⅓ cup natural unsweetened creamy peanut butter

Preheat the oven to 350°F. Lightly grease a 9-by-13-inch baking dish with cooking spray, then line it with parchment paper so the 2 longer paper edges overlap the dish edges by about 1 inch.

In a medium bowl, stir together the eggs, cocoa powder, baking powder, salt, and cayenne (if using); the mixture will be very thick.

In a saucepan over medium-low heat, melt the butter. Add the sugar and cook, stirring, until the mixture is shiny and bubbling and the sugar is somewhat dissolved, about 2 minutes. Pour the sugar mixture over the cocoa mixture and stir with a whisk until mostly smooth. Stir in the vanilla, then stir in the flour. Lastly, stir in the chocolate chips.

Spread the batter into the prepared baking dish in an even layer. Dollop the peanut butter all over the top, then use a knife to swirl it through the batter.

Bake the brownies until the edges and top look set and the brownies are just cooked through but still moist, about 30 minutes. Transfer the pan to a wire rack and let the brownies cool completely. Remove the brownies from the pan using the parchment "handles," then cut and serve.

"WHEN HER MOM WOULD GO ON A BROTH KICK, AMY WOULD COME OVER TO MY HOUSE, AND WE'D STUFF OURSELVES WITH BROWNIES."

—WILLOW
"WITCH" (SEASON 1, EPISODE 3)

MAKES 1½ QUARTS

Pineapple Panic Fro-Yo

This creamy and fresh pineapple frozen yogurt is light, tangy, and easy to love, unlike the college cafeteria's frozen yogurt machine, which Buffy accidentally breaks in front of Riley and his friends. While Forrest and Graham not-so-subtly comment on how hot she is, Buffy struggles to replace the handle midpour before tripping and dropping her hard-won frozen yogurt on the ground. Total cringe moment.

Ingredients

1 cup canned crushed pineapple, chilled

¾ cup cold pineapple juice

1½ cups whole milk plain yogurt

¾ cup heavy cream

½ cup sugar

2 tablespoons light corn syrup

1 teaspoon pure vanilla extract

Pinch kosher salt

Special Equipment

Ice cream maker

Blender

Freeze an ice cream canister for at least 24 hours before starting.

Put the pineapple, pineapple juice, yogurt, heavy cream, sugar, corn syrup, vanilla, and salt into a blender and blend until smooth. Pour into a bowl and refrigerate for at least 30 minutes or up to overnight.

Pour the mixture into an ice cream maker and churn according to the manufacturer's instructions. Spoon the finished frozen yogurt into an airtight freezer-safe container. Press parchment paper directly onto the surface of the frozen yogurt, cover, and freeze until a bit firmer, about 1 hour. Scoop and serve. (The fro-yo freezes hard, so let it sit at room temperature to soften before scooping.)

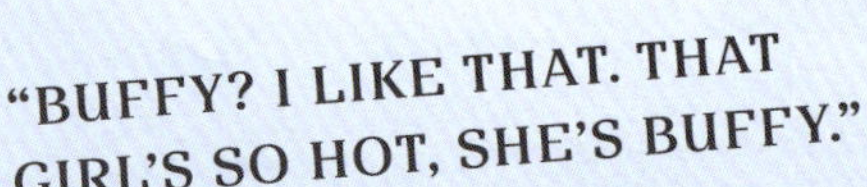

"BUFFY? I LIKE THAT. THAT GIRL'S SO HOT, SHE'S BUFFY."

—FORREST
"THE INITIATIVE" (SEASON 4, EPISODE 7)

WINNER GETS A GIFT CARD TO THE BRONZE

TALENT SHOW SIGN UP

NAME	TALENT
Emily	Ballet
Cordelia	Singing
Morgan	Puppetry
Marc	Magic!
Buffy, Xander, Willow	Please don't make us do this!

CHAPTER SIX

DEMON DRINKS

"SUNNYDALE: Come for the food, stay for the dismemberment."

—XANDER
"BENEATH YOU," (SEASON 7, EPISODE 2)

In a town where the nightlife often comes with actual fangs, it's good to have a drink in hand that won't leave you under some thrall-y spell. These nonalcoholic concoctions bubble, fizz, and sparkle enough to rival any cauldron, making them perfect for prepatrol hangouts, post-slay cooldowns, or keeping your cool when the demon across the room at the Bronze is giving you the evil eye.

MAKES 1 MOCKTAIL

Dark and Stormy Angel

Brooding, intense, and unexpectedly refreshing—this nonalcoholic mocktail channels the moody essence of Angel. With dark iced tea, spicy ginger beer, fresh lime, muddled blackberries, and mint, it's layered and complex, just like Buffy's most tortured love interest. Angel may have spent a century honing his guilt and avoiding the sunlight, but one sip of this drink, and you'll understand the pull. Serve over ice with a mint sprig, preferably while staring moodily into the middle distance.

Ingredients

4 fresh blackberries

3 fresh mint leaves, plus 1 small sprig for garnish

Juice of ½ lime

3 ounces cold black tea

5 ounces cold ginger beer (non-alcoholic)

Special Equipment

Cocktail shaker

Muddler

In a cocktail shaker, muddle 3 of the blackberries and the mint leaves and lime juice. Fill the shaker with ice and add the tea. Cover and shake vigorously until chilled. Strain into a tall glass filled with ice. Top with the ginger beer and gently stir with a bar spoon. Garnish with the remaining blackberry and the mint sprig and serve.

"THINGS USED TO BE PRETTY SIMPLE. A HUNDRED YEARS . . . JUST HANGING OUT, FEELING GUILTY . . . REALLY HONED MY BROODING SKILLS. THEN SHE COMES ALONG."

—ANGEL

"LIE TO ME" (SEASON 2, EPISODE 7)

MAKES 1 MOCKTAIL

Sacrificial Sunset

This layered drink, with orange and pineapple juice, lime, and a drizzle of grenadine, captures the fiery beauty of a sunset and the emotional weight of Buffy's greatest sacrifice. In "The Gift," in order to save Dawn and the world, Buffy leaps into the portal between dimensions, ending one life so another can begin. Like the final moments before dusk, this mocktail is bittersweet, radiant, and reflective of both loss and hope. Serve chilled and sip in quiet remembrance.

Ingredients

2 ounces freshly squeezed orange juice

2 ounces pineapple juice

½ ounce freshly squeezed lime juice

½ ounce grenadine

1 slice orange

1 chunk fresh pineapple

Fill a chilled wine glass or rocks glass with ice, then add the orange, pineapple, and lime juices. Stir gently with a bar spoon. Slowly pour the grenadine into the drink; it will sink to the bottom and create a layered effect. Spear the orange slice and pineapple chunk with a cocktail stick to garnish the drink.

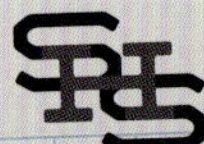

"GIVE MY LOVE TO MY FRIENDS. YOU HAVE TO TAKE CARE OF THEM NOW. YOU HAVE TO TAKE CARE OF EACH OTHER."

—BUFFY

"THE GIFT" (SEASON 5, EPISODE 22

MAKES 1 SHAKE

The Resurrection Scream

This nostalgic shake—blending vanilla ice cream and fresh orange flavors—is an ode to the bittersweet contrast of Buffy's return from the grave. Sweet and creamy on the surface, but with a sharp citrus bite that lingers underneath, it echoes the emotional dissonance she faces after being ripped from peaceful afterlife by well-meaning friends. Much like Buffy's rebirth into a world that feels too harsh and too bright, this shake is the familiar layered over something deeply unsettling.

Ingredients

3 large scoops vanilla ice cream

¾ cup freshly squeezed orange juice

¾ teaspoon pure vanilla extract

Whipped cream, for serving

Finely grated orange zest, for garnish

Special Equipment

Blender

Put the ice cream, orange juice, and vanilla into a blender. Cover and blend on medium-high speed until smooth. Pour into a milk shake glass or other tall glass. Top with whipped cream and sprinkle with orange zest. Serve.

"I THINK I WAS IN HEAVEN . . . AND NOW I'M NOT."

—BUFFY

"AFTER LIFE" (SEASON 6, EPISODE 3)

MAKES 1 MOCKTAIL

The Love Spell

This sparkling strawberry and rose water lemonade mocktail blends muddled berries, lemon juice, rose water, and a splash of magic, similar to the sweet rekindled connection between Willow and Tara. In a quiet dorm room lit only by candlelight, Willow assures Tara that she's where she belongs—with the one she loves. The soft fizz and floral notes of this drink are a tribute to love that endures, even after all the heartbreak and spells gone wrong. Swap out the strawberries for raspberries if you like.

Ingredients

2 fresh ripe strawberries, hulled and sliced, plus 1 small strawberry for garnish

Juice of ½ lemon

½ ounce simple syrup or agave nectar

¼ ounce rose water

4 ounces sparkling pink lemonade

Lemon twist, for garnish

Special Equipment

Cocktail shaker

Muddler

In a cocktail shaker, muddle the sliced strawberries and lemon juice. Fill the shaker with ice and add the simple syrup and rose water. Cover and shake until chilled. Strain into a rocks glass filled with ice. Top with the sparkling pink lemonade and gently stir with a bar spoon. Garnish with the lemon twist and the small strawberry and serve.

"LIFE WAS STARTING TO GET SO GOOD AGAIN, AND...YOU'RE A BIG PART OF THAT. AND HERE COMES THE THING I WANTED MOST OF ALL, AND . . . I DON'T KNOW WHAT TO DO."

—WILLOW
"NEW MOON RISING" (SEASON 4, EPISODE 19)

MAKES 1 MOCKTAIL

Bronze Brew

Ah, the Bronze—Sunnydale's favorite all-ages hangout. This spicy, refreshing nonalcoholic michelada is quintessentially the Bronze: the perfect drink for dancing with your Slayerettes, jamming out to the latest Dingoes Ate My Baby song, or just casually chatting before kicking some vampire butt. With crisp nonalcoholic beer, tangy lime, savory tomato juice, and a dash of hot sauce, it's bold, fun, and a little unpredictable—much like a night out in the Hellmouth's hot spot. This brew brings the flavor without the buzz.

Ingredients

3 lime wedges

1 teaspoon Tajín seasoning

3 ounces tomato juice

1 teaspoon hot pepper sauce

½ teaspoon Worcestershire sauce

One 12-ounce can nonalcoholic lager-style or light beer

Rub the rim of a chilled pint glass with 1 lime wedge. Spread the Tajín seasoning on a saucer and dip the rim of the glass in the seasoning to coat the edges. Fill the glass two-thirds full of ice.

Add the tomato juice, hot pepper sauce, and Worcestershire sauce to the glass. Squeeze a second lime wedge into the tomato juice, then drop it in. Stir gently with a bar spoon. Top with the nonalcoholic beer and stir gently. Garnish with the remaining lime wedge on the rim and serve, with the rest of the beer alongside for topping up as you go.

"IT'S THE ONLY CLUB WORTH GOING TO AROUND HERE. THEY LET ANYBODY IN, BUT IT'S STILL THE SCENE. IT'S IN THE BAD PART OF TOWN."

—CORDELIA
"WELCOME TO THE HELLMOUTH"
(SEASON 1, EPISODE 1)

DINGOES

ATE MY BABY

About the Author

KIM LAIDLAW is a *New York Times* best-selling cookbook author, recipe developer, and editor. She is the author or coauthor of over twenty cookbooks, including best sellers *Elvira's Cookbook from Hell*, *Yellowstone: The Official Dutton Ranch Family Cookbook*, *Tim Burton's The Nightmare Before Christmas: The Official Cookbook*, *Emily in Paris: The Official Cookbook* along with *Clueless: The Official Cookbook* and *The Rocky Horror Cookbook*. She has also authored numerous Williams Sonoma cookbooks. Kim is a seasoned recipe developer and tester who works with international brands, celebrities, chefs, influencers, and authors. Her clients include Paramount, Netflix, Disney, Samuel Adams, Weber, American Girl, and more. She has managed hundreds of cookbook projects, including 2025 James Beard award winner *Convivir*, and Kendall-Jackson's *Season*, winner of the 2019 International Association of Culinary Professionals Book of the Year award. She is a former professional baker and baking instructor at the San Francisco Cooking School and attended the California Culinary Academy.

Measurement Conversions

CUPS	TABLESPOONS	TEASPOONS	FLUID OUNCES
1⁄16 cup	1 tablespoon	3 teaspoons	½ fluid ounce
1⁄8 cup	2 tablespoons	6 teaspoons	1 fluid ounce
¼ cup	4 tablespoons	12 teaspoons	2 fluid ounces
⅓ cup	5½ tablespoons	16 teaspoons	2⅔ fluid ounces
½ cup	8 tablespoons	24 teaspoons	4 fluid ounces
⅔ cup	10⅔ tablespoons	32 teaspoons	5⅓ fluid ounces
¾ cup	12 tablespoons	36 teaspoons	6 fluid ounces
1 cup	16 tablespoons	48 teaspoons	8 fluid ounces

GALLONS	QUARTS	PINTS	CUPS	FLUID OUNCES
1⁄16 gallon	¼ quart	½ pint	1 cup	8 fluid ounces
1⁄8 gallon	½ quart	1 pint	2 cups	16 fluid ounces
¼ gallon	1 quart	2 pints	4 cups	32 fluid ounces
½ gallon	2 quarts	4 pints	8 cups	64 fluid ounces
1 gallon	4 quarts	8 pints	16 cups	128 fluid ounces

GRAMS	OUNCES
14 grams	½ ounce
28 grams	1 ounce
57 grams	2 ounces
85 grams	3 ounces
113 grams	4 ounces
142 grams	5 ounces
170 grams	6 ounces
283 grams	10 ounces
397 grams	14 ounces
454 grams	16 ounces
907 grams	32 ounces

IMPERIAL	METRIC
1 inch	2.5 centimeters
2 inches	5 centimeters
4 inches	10 centimeters
6 inches	15 centimeters
8 inches	20 centimeters
10 inches	25 centimeters
12 inches	30 centimeters

FAHRENHEIT	CELSIUS
200°F	93°C
225°F	107°C
250°F	121°C
275°F	135°C
300°F	149°C
325°F	163°C
350°F	177°C
375°F	191°C
400°F	204°C
425°F	218°C
450°F	232°C

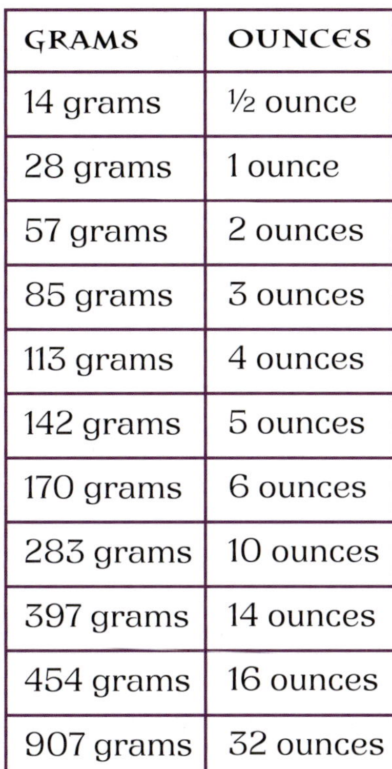

INDEX

D

E

F

G

H

I

J

L

M

N

O

P

R

S

T

V

W

Y

Z

PO Box 3088
San Rafael, CA 94912
www.insighteditions.com

Find us on Facebook: www.facebook.com/InsightEditions
Follow us on Instagram: @insighteditions

ISBN: 979-8-3374-0149-2

Publisher: Raoul Goff
SVP, Group Publisher: Vanessa Lopez
VP, Manufacturing: Alix Nicholaeff
Associate Publisher: Thom O'Hearn
Art Director: Stuart Smith
Senior Designer: Brooke McCullum
Senior Editor: Eileen Mullan
Editorial Assistant: Melissa Santoyo
Managing Editor: Shannon Ballesteros
Production Editor: Ivy Long
Production Manager: Deena Hashem
Strategic Production Planner: Lina s Palma-Temena

Photography by Waterbury Publications, Inc.

ROOTS of PEACE REPLANTED PAPER

Insight Editions, in association with Roots of Peace, will plant two trees for each tree used in the manufacturing of this book. Roots of Peace is an internationally renowned humanitarian organization dedicated to eradicating land mines worldwide and converting war-torn lands into productive farms and wildlife habitats. Roots of Peace will plant two million fruit and nut trees in Afghanistan and provide farmers there with the skills and support necessary for sustainable land use.

Manufactured in China by Insight Editions

10 9 8 7 6 5 4 3 2 1